**Illustrator:**
Barb Lorseyedi

**Editor:**
Stephanie Buehler, M.P.W., M.A.

**Editorial Project Manager:**
Ina Massler Levin, M.A.

**Editor in Chief:**
Sharon Coan, M.S. Ed.

**Art Director:**
Elayne Roberts

**Associate Designer:**
Denise Bauer

**Cover Artist:**
Sue Fullam

**Product Manager:**
Phil Garcia

**Imaging:**
David Bennett
Pete Sadony

**Publishers:**
Rachelle Cracchiolo, M.S. Ed.
Mary Dupuy Smith, M.S. Ed.

# Learning Throug~~h~~ S0-EAQ-769

# Ecology

## INTERMEDIATE

**Authors:**

*Liz Rothlein, Ed. D.*

*Sharon Vaughn, Ph. D.*

*Teacher Created Materials, Inc.*
P.O. Box 1040
Huntington Beach, CA   92647
**ISBN-1-55734-475-2**

©*1996 Teacher Created Materials, Inc.*          Made in U.S.A.

**Teacher Created Materials**

# Table of Contents

# Introduction

The world we live in provides technology, transportation, and resources that give us previously unknown comforts and conveniences. Unfortunately, these advancements come with a price, and that price is environmental damage, waste, and destruction. Many people fear that the world as we know it will be substantially changed over the next 20 years unless we all make enormous changes now. Perhaps our greatest hope for initiating and sustaining these changes is through our children. As teachers and parents, we have the opportunity and responsibility to inform them about the environment so that they can respond effectively and appropriately.

This book has been developed to address the learning needs of students in Grades 3 through 5, although our experience shows a broader grade range can enjoy and learn from the children's books and activities. *Learning Through Literature: Ecology* can be used by teachers and parents as a resource for background knowledge and planned lessons to teach children what they need to know to improve the environment. Our intention is that after reading the suggested books and completing the activities, every student will be able to answer two questions: (1) What can I do to make a difference in protecting our planet Earth? and (2) What can I do to alter the pattern of destruction?

To address these questions, we have divided this guide into four sections: **Our Good Earth, Pollution, Endangered Species,** and **Forests.** It is not necessary to cover the sections in any particular order, although we suggest completing an entire section before proceeding to another.

The title, author, and publisher of each selected children's book is provided within each lesson. A brief summary of the book's content, as well as a pre-reading activity, is suggested. Key concepts are identified, and there are questions and answers related to the book's content. Finally, ideas are provided for activity sheets, assignments, and group work related to the topic. We refer to these activities as "connecting activities" because they connect the book content with core academic content such as literature, spelling, mathematics, social studies, science, and humanities.

We hope you and your students enjoy this book. Even more importantly, we hope that after reading the books and participating in the activities that you and your students are better informed caretakers of our environment.

# Our Good Earth

# Alejandro's Gift

**Author:** Richard E. Albert

**Illustrator:** Sylvia Long

**Publisher:** Chronicle Books, 1994.

**Summary:** Alejandro is an old man who lives in a small adobe house in the Southwestern desert with only a burro for a companion. He plants a garden and becomes acquainted with the desert animals. He then gives his wide circle of desert friends the gift of the water hole.

## Pre-reading Activity

Ask the children what they think the desert is like in the Southwestern part of the United States. Is it just a lot of sand? Are there any plants and animals that live in the desert? Show them the picture of Alejandro's desert home on the first page of the book and discuss what is shown.

## Key Concepts:

- desert
- water hole
- windmill

- tortoise
- burro
- bobcat

- javelina
- adobe
- coati

## Post-reading Questions

1. Why did Alejandro start his garden? *(He wanted to have something to do.)*

2. What was Alejandro's first visitor? How did the visitor make him feel? *(Alejandro's first visitor was a ground squirrel. Alejandro felt less lonely.)*

3. Alejandro did not think only of himself. He wondered what his desert friends needed. What was it? *(He realized the animals were coming to drink the water that he was using to irrigate his garden.)*

# Alejandro's Gift (cont.)

## Post-reading Questions (cont.)

4. How many animals can you name that came to visit Alejandro? *(ground squirrels, wood rats, pocket gophers, jackrabbits, kangaroo rats, pocket mice, roadrunners, Gila woodpeckers, thrashers, cactus wrens, sage sparrows, mourning doves, a desert tortoise, coyotes, desert gray foxes, bobcats, skunks, badgers, coatis, javelinas, and mule deer)*

## Learning Activities

• In *Alejandro's Gift,* we are introduced to many interesting desert animals, birds, and plants. The animals, birds, and plants of the desert sheet on page seven lists several animals, birds, and plants from the book. Write a brief description next to each one.

• On the first day of the story, Alejandro saw only one type of animal. Then, he saw one additional type of animal every day for the next 15 days. On day 15, how many types of animals were coming to his garden? *(Answer: 15)* What was the total number of animals he saw over the 15-day period?

*(Answer: 1 + 2 + 3 + 4 + 5 + 6 + 7 + 8 + 9 + 10 + 11 + 12 + 13 + 14 + 15 = 120)*

• Facts and questions about the largest deserts in the world are found on page 9.

• Cacti are found only in American deserts. The tallest cactus is the saguaro, which can reach 50 feet and weigh up to seven tons. On art paper, ask students to draw a saguaro cactus. Include a proportionally-sized person to show the cactus' relative height. Students may also draw smaller cacti and trees located in the Sonoran Desert; label them.

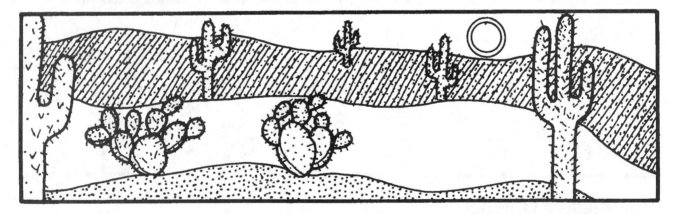

• The Sahara Desert is nearly as big as the entire United States. Locate the Sahara Desert on a map. Notice that its area makes up almost one-third of Africa. To what other continents or countries can the Sahara Desert be compared? Make at least five comparisons between the Sahara Desert and other countries and continents.

• The Atacama Desert, located in northern Chile, is the driest place on Earth. There exist places in this desert where no rain has fallen for 400 years (1570–1971) and where no rain has ever been recorded. Use library books to learn more about the Atacama Desert and then list five to ten facts about it.

**Name** _____ **Date** _____

# Animals, Birds, and Plants of the Desert

**Directions:** Next to each listed animal, bird, or plant, write a brief description. For the animals and birds, tell what foods they like to eat.

## Animals of the Desert

**Arizona pocket mouse** _____

_____

**badger** _____

_____

**bobcat** _____

_____

**rabbit** _____

_____

**gopher** _____

_____

**desert tortoise** _____

_____

**coyote** _____

_____

**collared peccary** _____

_____

**kangaroo rat** _____

_____

**mule deer** _____

_____

**Name** _____ **Date** _____

# Animals, Birds, and Plants
# of the Desert *(cont.)*

## Birds of the Desert

**cactus wren** _____

_____

**elf owl** _____

_____

**hummingbird** _____

_____

**quail** _____

_____

**roadrunner** _____

_____

**sparrow** _____

_____

**dove** _____

_____

## Plants of the Desert

**saguaro** _____

_____

**mesquite** _____

_____

**ocotillo** _____

_____

**prickly pear** _____

_____

**paloverde** _____

_____

**Name** _____**Date**_____

# Deserts of the World

Directions: Use the table below to answer the questions about deserts of the world.

## The World's Largest Deserts

| Deserts | Location | Size ($Km^2$) |
|---|---|---|
| Namib | Southwest Africa | 1,300,000 |
| Arabian | Southwest Asia | 2,300,000 |
| Australian | Australia | 3,367,000 |
| Gobi | Central Asia | 1,295,000 |
| Kalahari | South Africa | 450,000 |
| Patagonia | South America | 673,400 |
| Sahara | North Africa | 9,000,000 |
| Sonora | USA/Mexico | 320,000 |
| Takla Makan | China | 337,600 |
| Turkestan | Central Asia | 450,000 |

1. In order of size from largest to smallest, list the names of the five largest deserts. _____

   _____

2. List the deserts that are found in Asia._____

   _____

3. List the deserts that are found in North America._____

   _____

4. List the deserts that are less than 500,000 square kilometers in area._____

   _____

5. Add together the area of all deserts that are smaller than the Sahara.  Is the total area of these deserts greater than or less than the total area of the Sahara? _____

   _____

6. List the deserts found in Africa. What is the total area of those deserts? _____

   _____

# *Walden*

**Author:** Henry David Thoreau

**Illustrator:** Robert Sabuda

**Publisher:** Philomel Books, 1990.

**Summary:** This picture book, *Walden*, consists of actual excerpts from Thoreau's famous book, *Walden* plus wonderful linoleum-cut illustrations. *Walden* describes Thoreau's life as he built a cabin in the woods and lived beside Walden Pond in Massachusetts, close to nature, for two years. *On Walden Pond* has become a great nature classic.

## Pre-reading Activity

Tell the children that 150 years ago few people were interested in nature or the environment. One man, Henry David Thoreau, built a cabin in the woods and lived there alone. Many people felt that this was a very strange thing to do. What do you think? Why do you think someone would choose to live alone?

## Key Concepts:

- New England
- horizon
- mythology
- solitude
- society
- pirouetting
- whip-poor-will
- North Star
- morning star

## Post-Reading Questions

1. How long did it take Thoreau to build his cabin? Do you think you could build a cabin in the woods with just a few tools? *(He started building late in March and moved in on the fourth of July.)*

2. Thoreau said that when he was gardening, he was making the earth "say beans instead of grass." What did he mean? *(He meant, of course, that now beans would grow there instead of grass—something that could be eaten rather than something ornamental. The earth did not actually speak; Thoreau used a metaphor.)*

3. Thoreau said, "I am no more lonely than ... the north star." Does this means he is or is not lonely? Explain your thoughts.

4. Do you think Thoreau was or was not a well-educated man? Why? *(In fact, Thoreau graduated from Harvard University in 1837 and had studied six different languages.)*

5. What do you think *Walden* teaches us? *(Answers may vary.)*

# *Walden* (cont.)

## Learning Activities

- Ask students to solve the following math problems about Henry David Thoreau.

  - *Thoreau was born in 1817. How old would he be if he were still alive today? (Answers will vary depending on the current year.)*

  - *He graduated from Harvard in 1837. How old was he then? (20)*
  *When his brother, John, died in 1842, they had been teaching school together for several years. How old was Thoreau when his brother died? (25)*

  - *Henry David Thoreau would occasionally sit in his doorway from sunrise until noon, undisturbed, listening to the birds sing or watching them flit around. About how many hours do you think he sat there? How long are you able to sit still, quietly listening and watching something? (Answers will vary.)*

Henry David Thoreau

- Based on the following quote from Thoreau, draw a picture of what you think Walden Pond must have looked like. "Already, by the first of September, I have seen two or three small maples turn scarlet across the pond . . . and gradually, from week to week, the character of each tree came out, and it admired itself reflected in the smooth mirror of the lake."

- Using page 12, ask students to make a list of the sounds that Henry David Thoreau discussed in his book and then categorize them either as natural or made by humans.

- After two years, Henry David Thoreau left Walden Pond. Direct students to make up a story to describe what Thoreau did during the next two years of his life.

- Thoreau had no running water during the two years he lived at Walden Pond. He used the pond water for drinking, cooking, bathing, and laundering—but he did not waste a drop. However, there are many ways in which we waste water. One major source of water waste is a dripping faucet. Complete page 14 to find out about the effects of a dripping faucet.

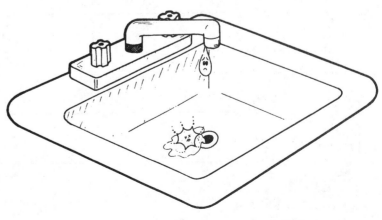

**Name** _____ **Date** _____

# Natural and Unnatural Noises

**Directions:** List the noises that Henry David Thoreau heard while he was living near Walden Pond. Categorize each noise as natural or man-made. The first two have been done for you.

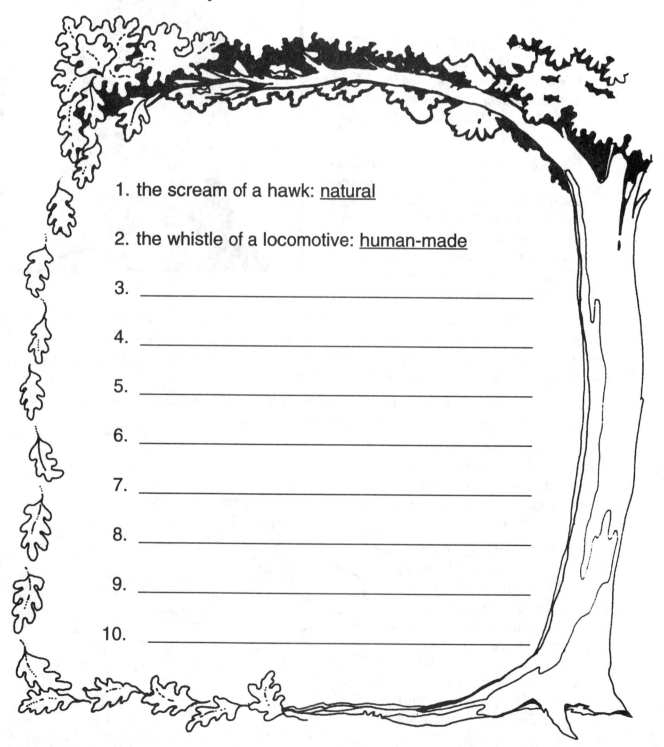

1. the scream of a hawk: <u>natural</u>

2. the whistle of a locomotive: <u>human-made</u>

3. _____

4. _____

5. _____

6. _____

7. _____

8. _____

9. _____

10. _____

**Name** _____ **Date** _____

# After Walden Pond

**Directions:** Read the quote, below, from Henry David Thoreau explaining why he left Walden Pond. Then, create a story that describes what Henry David Thoreau did during the two years after he left Walden Pond.

> *I left the woods for as good a reason as I went there. Perhaps it seemed to me that I had several more lives to live, and could not spare any more time for that one.*

_____

_____

_____

_____

_____

_____

_____

_____

_____

_____

_____

_____

_____

**Name** _____**Date**_____

# Drip Drop

**Directions:** Complete the experiment below and then answer the questions that follow.

**Experiment:**

Place a large cup or bowl under a faucet in your bathroom. Turn on the faucet so that the water will drip slowly into the bowl or cup. Using a watch with a second hand or a timer, stand by the dripping faucet and count how many seconds it takes to fill the bowl or cup. Then, answer the following questions.

1. How long did it take to fill the cup or bowl?

   _____

2. How many ounces/milliliters of water does it take to fill your cup or bowl? Use a measuring cup; remember, there are 8 ounces/245 mL in a cup.

   _____

3. If your faucet leaked at the same rate for five minutes, how many cups or bowls of water would be wasted?

   _____

4. Look inside and outside your house or apartment building. How many faucets do you have altogether?

   _____

5. Check each faucet carefully. Are any of them dripping?

   _____

6. Work with your parents to take care that all your faucets are turned off and that all of you use water sparingly. Describe what you have done.

   _____

   _____

   _____

   _____

   _____

# What Do We Know About Grasslands?

**Author:** Brian Knapp

**Publisher:** Peter Bedrick Books, 1992.

**Summary:** This book describes the nature, location, and the use of the great grasslands of the earth. It shows how people have exploited grasslands throughout history and discusses ways the few remaining grasslands may be saved.

## Pre-reading Activity

Many people live in one of the world's grasslands. Much of the Middle West of the United States is a grassland area. Show the children the map on the first pages of the book. Do you live in such an area, or have you ever visited one? What does it look like now?

## Key Concepts:

- prairies
- desert
- arid
- browsers

- savannas
- rain forest
- monsoon
- carnivores

- steppes
- humid
- drought
- cultivation

## Post-reading Questions

1. The prairies of the United States, which are a type of temperate-region grassland, have experienced much change in the last one hundred years. In what ways have they changed? *(They used to be made up of miles and miles of prairie grass. They were inhabited by buffalo and nomadic Native Americans. Now many are planted with wheat or corn or used for grazing.)*

# What Do We Know About Grasslands? *(cont.)*

## Post-reading Questions *(cont.)*

2. Why are trees rarely found on grasslands? *(Droughts and fires that are common in grasslands make it difficult for trees to survive.)*

3. What is the most important factor that aided use of grasslands by farmers and ranchers? *(Railroads provided the transportation necessary to get farm products to market, making it economically worthwhile to exploit grasslands.)*

4. What happens when prairies and savannas are farmed by primitive methods? *(The soil quickly becomes exhausted and easily eroded. Wind blows dry soil away, leading to "dust bowls," and water runoff washes the topsoil away, ruining the land.)*

5. Large tracts of savanna still exist. What economic factor may save them from being cultivated like the prairies? *(Savannahs support exotic wildlife, such as elephants, leopards, and lions. Tourists will pay money to visit savannas if these areas are made into wildlife parks.)*

## Learning Activities

- Ask students to do page 17 by completing each sentence with the appropriate word from the vocabulary box.

- Grasslands and savannahs are not called the same thing in all parts of the world. A list of countries and the names they use for the grassland or savannah is provided on page 18. Look up each name in the dictionary or encyclopedia and see what definition is provided. Discuss with students the fact that one of the greatest threats to grasslands and savannahs is fire. Ask them to provide a list of the dangers from fire to grasslands and savannahs. How well do grasslands and savannas recover?

- Products developed from wild grasses are identified on page 19. After the name of each grass, have students list several foods made from these grasses.

- Pictures and matching word cards are printed on page 20. For example, the elephant goes with the phrase the "largest animal on the savannah." Direct students to cut out the cards and play concentration. Whoever has the most pairs at the end of the game wins.

- Complete page 21 to identify whether the animals listed live on a grassland or a savannah. Direct students to also tell what each animal needs to survive.

**Name** _____ **Date** _____

# Grassland Vocabulary

**Directions:** Match each of the words in the box with one of the definitions that follow.  Write the word on the blank line.

> - carnivores
> - predator
> - prairie
> - monsoon
> - herbivores
> - decomposers
> - arid region
> - savannah

1. A region of grass and scattered trees that is located in the tropics

   _____

2. A wet, rainy season that occurs in some areas bordering the tropics

   _____

3. An animal that preys on or hunts another animal for food

   _____

4. A region of cool, temperate grassland that is too dry for trees to dominate

   _____

5. Animals that require meat to live

   _____

6. Animals that require plants to live

   _____

7. Animals and insects that eat dead tissue and return nutrients to the soil

   _____

8. A region that has low, unpredictable rainfall

   _____

Name _____ Date _____

# What Is My Name?

**Directions:** Listed below are countries and the term each has to refer to grasslands and savannas. Look up the names in an encyclopedia and write a brief description of the area named. Check to see if it meets the criteria for grasslands or savannas provided in *What Do We Know About Grasslands?*

| Country | Name | Description |
|---|---|---|
| **North America** | prairie | |
| **Argentina** | pampas | |
| **South Africa** | veldt | |
| **Australia** | scrub | |
| **Central Asia** | steppes | |
| **Brazil** | campo | |
| **East Africa** | savanna | |
| **Venezuela** | llanos | |

**Name** _____**Date**_____

# From Wild Grasses to Cereals

**Directions:** Listed below are the names of cereals that have been developed from wild grasses.  Identify at least two products that are made from these developed grasses.

1. Wheat _____

_____

2. Rice _____

_____

3. Oats _____

_____

4. Millet _____

_____

5. Maize _____

_____

6. Rye _____

_____

7. Barley _____

_____

8. Sorghum _____

_____

**Name** _____ **Date** _____

# Grassland Conservation

See directions on page 16.

| | | |
|---|---|---|
| Elephant | | The largest animal on the savannah |
| Native American Tepee | | Prairie |
| Buffalo | | Bison on the prairie |
| Baobab Tree | | The upside down tree |
| Giraffe | | Grazer |
| Grasslands | | Treeless |
| Cereal | | Wheat |
| Irrigation | | Providing needed water |

**Name** _____**Date**_____

# Where Do I Live?

**Directions:** Each animal listed below lives on a prairie or a savanna. Beside each animal's name, indicate where the animal lives and what it needs to keep from becoming extinct.

| Animal | Animal Habitat | Prevent Extinction |
|---|---|---|
| 1. Elephant | | |
| 2. Bison | | |
| 3. Giraffe | | |
| 4. Leopard | | |
| 5. Coyote | | |
| 6. Prairie Dog | | |
| 7. Antelope | | |

# Earth Book for Kids

**Author:** Linda Schwartz

**Illustrator:** Beverly Armstrong

**Publisher:** The Learning Works, Inc., 1990.

**Summary:** *Earth Book for Kids* provides many worthwhile, enjoyable environmental activities for children, as well as their families. The book will acquaint readers with their environment and suggest how to care for it.

## Pre-reading Activity

Read the book's title and then ask students to predict what the book is about. Have students record their predictions in individual environmental journals which they can add to as they proceed through this unit. Allow time to share and discuss journals.

## Key Concepts:

- solar energy
- topsoil
- wetlands

- acid rain
- carnivores
- aqueduct

- deforestation
- herbivores
- pesticide residue

## Post-reading Questions

1. After reviewing the information in this book, what do you think are the biggest environmental problems facing your community? Your state? Your country? *(Answers may vary.)*

2. Do you think people in your community are aware of all the problems facing the environment today? Explain. *(Answers may vary.)*

3. What do you think is the most important thing you can do to help save planet Earth? *(Answers may vary.)*

4. Why are people interested in writing books about saving the environment? *(Answers may vary.)*

5. What is the most important message conveyed by this book? *(Answers may vary.)*

# Earth Book for Kids *(cont.)*

## Learning Activities

- As a group, write a letter to the author, Linda Schwartz, via the publisher. Include in your letter what you liked about the book and how it has helped, or will help, you to care more about the environment. Be creative about other things to communicate to her.

- There are many poems throughout this book, including a haiku on page 111 and two poems written by children on pages 183 and 184. Ask the students to read some of these poems and then to write a poem that relates to preserving our environment, using page 24. Display the poems and then compile them into a class book.

- Ask the students to make a list of things in their immediate environment that they think need attention (page 25). Then, as a group, categorize the list and use pages 132–137 in *Earth Book for Kids* as a guide to develop a plan of action for helping to solve the identified environmental problems. Ask several students to act as recorders during the project, recording the progress being made, changes you might make, goals you have achieved, etc.

- Ask the students to work in pairs to create a full-page advertisement for the local or school newspaper about preserving the environment (page 26). As a class, decide which ad best gets the message across and submit it to your local newspaper.

- Divide the class into three groups correlating with chapters in *Earth Book for Kids*: Energy, Resources, and Recycling; Air, Land, and Water; Plant and Animal Habitats. Then, allow students time and space to create a booth or display area for an exhibit of resources and information relating to their topic. Encourage them to write to some of the resources provided in the glossary of the book. This activity may be ongoing over several weeks or a month.

- On the cover of the book, one of the children is wearing a shirt that says "Save the Whales." The other child has a sign about litter and recycling. Ask the students to design something, for example, a shirt, bumper sticker, arm band or headband, etc., that contains a message about saving the environment.

**Name** _____**Date** _____

# Environmental Poetry

Directions: After reviewing the poems in *Earth Book for Kids*, write your own poem on a topic related to saving the environment.  Use lines below.  When you are finished, create an illustration to accompany your poem.

_____

_____

_____

_____

_____

_____

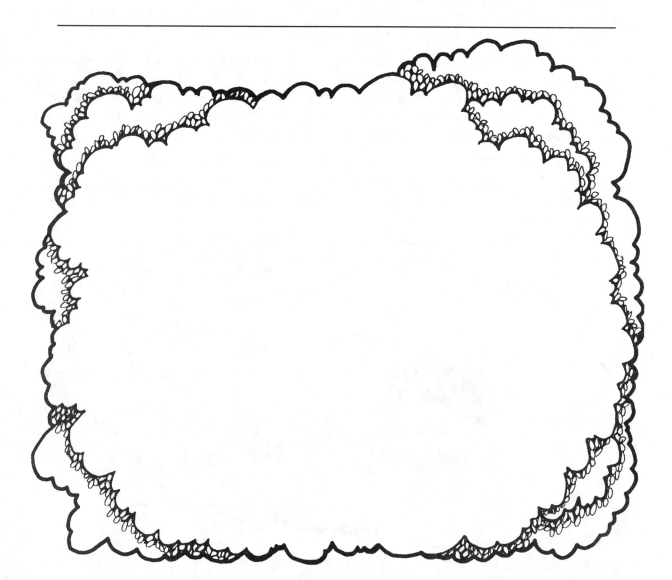

**Name** _____**Date** _____

# Environmental Problems and Solutions

**Directions:** List all the environmental problems in your home, school, and community that need attention.  Describe what you think needs to be done to help solve these problems.

Problems

_____

_____

_____

_____

_____

_____

_____

_____

Solutions

_____

_____

_____

_____

_____

_____

_____

_____

**Name** _____**Date**_____

# Eye-Catching Ads

**Directions:** Work with a classmate to create a full-page newspaper advertisement about an environmental concern. Study newspaper ads that are eye catching before you begin.

# Going Green: A Kid's Handbook to Saving the Planet

**Authors:** John Elkington, Julia Hailes, Douglas Hill, Joel Makower

**Illustrator:** Tony Ross

**Publisher:** Puffin Books, 1990.

**Summary:** *Going Green* provides children a guide for saving the environment and includes explanations of ecological issues and projects. Many facts about the environment, as well as suggestions for getting involved in saving the environment, are provided.

## Pre-reading Activity

Read aloud page 5 of *Going Green*, entitled "You Can Do It," to the students. Record the students' answers to the question, "So, what are you going to do?" Keep the list and refer to it several weeks later to follow up on what the students have done.

## Key Concepts:

- aerosols
- biodegradability
- disposable
- green consumerism

- energy efficient
- landfills
- pesticides
- global warming

- organic
- solid waste
- hazardous waste
- polystyrene

## Post-reading Questions

1. What do you see as the biggest problem facing the planet? Explain. *(Answers may vary.)*

2. What is the most interesting fact provided in this book? *(Answers may vary.)*

3. Has this book changed the way you feel about the environment? Why or why not? *(Answers may vary.)*

4. What one thing do you think you could do that would help save the environment? Explain why you think this would help. *(Answers may vary.)*

5. Would you recommend this book to a friend? Why or why not? *(Answers may vary.)*

# *Going Green: A Kid's Handbook to Saving the Planet* (cont.)

## Learning Activities

- With the students, review the A-to-Z list of "Things You Can Do" on pages 73–96 in *Going Green*. Then, ask the students on page 29 to create their own A-to-Z list of ways to help save the environment in their own communities.

- Ask the students to select one of the topics presented in *Going Green,* such as the ozone layer, acid rain, air pollution, greenhouse effect, etc. Then, ask them to use the facts in the book, as well as other information they find, to create a fact-filled flyer on page 30. Distribute the flyers in your community.

- The second part of *Going Green* is divided into sections entitled "How Green Is Your Home?" "How Green Is Your School" and "How Green Is Your Community?" Discuss what is meant by these questions. Then, divide the students into three groups and assign each a question. Ask the students to create a survey or audit that could be conducted to answer the question. Allow time for students to implement the survey with an appropriate group of people. Compile the data and share findings for each question.

- Ask students to select one environmental issue as a target project in which they can become involved. Then, tell them to design a plan of action that would provide assistance with the project. See the illustration at the right for an example.

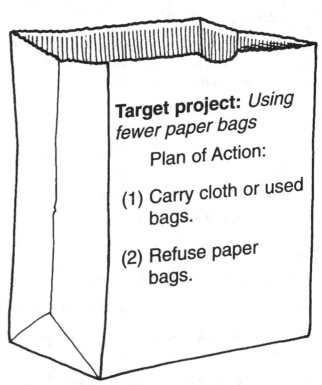

**Target project:** *Using fewer paper bags*

Plan of Action:

(1) Carry cloth or used bags.

(2) Refuse paper bags.

- On pages 98–100 of *Going Green* is a list of recommended books. As a class, try to collect as many of these and other books as you can to create an environmental section of books in your class or school library. Your class may also want to write to some of the organizations on pages 101–104 to request free or inexpensive materials.

- As a class, write a letter as requested on page 105 of *Going Green.* As a class project and calculate how much paper is used by the class in one day. (See pages 59 and 60 of *Going Green*).

**Name** _____ **Date** _____

# The Environment from A to Z

**Directions:** Create an A-to-Z list of things you can do to help save the environment. For example:

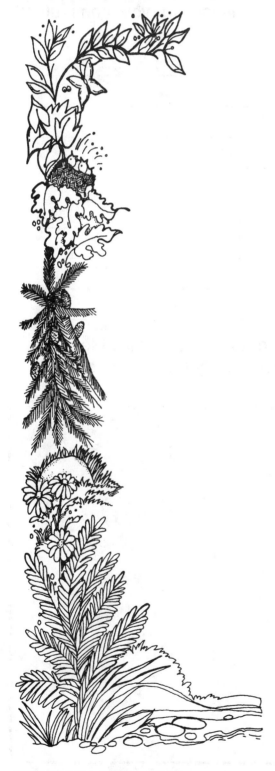

A - Always turn water off when not using it.

B - Be sure to throw trash in trash cans provided.

C - Collect newspapers to recycle.

A - _____

B - _____

C - _____

D - _____

E - _____

F - _____

G - _____

H - _____

I - _____

J - _____

K - _____

L - _____

M - _____

N - _____

O - _____

P - _____

Q - _____

R - _____

S - _____

T - _____

U - _____

V - _____

W - _____

X - _____

Y - _____

Z - _____

**Name** _____**Date** _____

# Create an Environmental Flyer

**Directions:** Select a topic or problem such as the greenhouse effect, air pollution, acid rain, hazardous waste, etc. Use that topic or problem as the basis of a flyer to create awareness and generate solutions for your community.

**Topic or Problem to Identify**

_____

_____

_____

_____

**Solutions to Suggest**

_____

_____

_____

_____

Draw a draft of your flyer here and then draw it on art paper. If possible, duplicate the flyers and distribute them in your community (but do not create waste).

# The Big Book for Our Planet

**Authors:** Ann Durell, Jean Craighead George, and Katherine Paterson

**Illustrator:** Jane Byers Bierhorst

**Publisher:** Dutton Children's Book, 1993.

**Summary:** This book contains nearly thirty stories and poems about environmental related issues. The stories and poems are written and illustrated by leading authors and illustrators of children's books. They have agreed to give the sale proceeds from the book to six environmental organizations.

## Pre-reading Activity

Read the book's title and the introduction to the students. Explain that many leading authors and illustrators of children's books contributed to this book and tell them where the proceeds will be going. Ask students for their reactions to this concept.

## Key Concepts:

- hyphae
- plague
- species
- habitats
- conservancy
- Audubon Society
- recycled matte paper
- Sturnus vulgaris

## Post-Reading Questions

1. Which of the poems in *The Big Book for Our Planet* do you think conveys the most important message? Which story? Explain. (*Answers may vary.*)

2. Why did such an outstanding group of authors/illustrators decide to pool their talents to write a book such as this? (*Answers may vary but might include because they care about the planet and they wanted to help make money to donate to six environmental organizations*).

# The Big Book for Our Planet *(cont.)*

## Post-Reading Questions *(cont.)*

3. What topics related to saving the planet were not addressed in the poems and stories included in this book? *(Answers may vary.)*

4. How do you think the book's contributors decided which environmental organizations to donate their royalty proceeds to? *(Answers may vary.)*

5. What did you learn from this book that would help you in saving the environment? *(Answers may vary.)*

6. Would you recommend this book to a friend? Why or why not? *(Answers may vary.)*

## Learning Activities

- As a class project, create your own *The Big Book for Our Planet* by asking each student to contribute a poem or short story about the environment. Compile the students' work into a book.

- *The Big Book for Our Planet* is written by over forty well-known authors and illustrators of children's books. Ask the students to select six stories or poems they like best in this book, identify the author and/or illustrator, and then list other books or poems written by that person (page 33). Collect as many of these works as possible for students to peruse.

- Tell the students to select one of the stories or poems in this book and create a book cover for it (page 34). The book jacket should include a summary of the story and information about the authors and/or illustrators. Display the jackets and allow students time to share.

- Tell the students to create an advertisement for their school or local newspaper in which they advertise *The Big Book for Our Planet* (page 35). If possible, make copies available to sell the book to interested people.

- Introduce various poetry forms, e.g., limericks, haiku, cinquain, etc. Then, ask the students to select one of the poetry forms and to work in pairs or small groups to write a poem about the environment and illustrate it. Display the poems.

- Ask the students to describe the stories and poems, using page 36. Allow time to discuss the adjectives they selected.

**Name** _____**Date** _____

# Six Picks

**Directions:** Select six of your favorite stories and/or poems and list them below. Identify the author or illustrator and then list other stories or poems written by that person.

| | |
|---|---|
| Story or Poem _____ <br><br> _____ <br><br> Author and/or Illustrator _____ <br><br> _____ <br><br> More Stories and/or Poems _____ <br><br> _____ <br><br> _____ | Story or Poem _____ <br><br> _____ <br><br> Author and/or Illustrator _____ <br><br> _____ <br><br> More Stories and/or Poems _____ <br><br> _____ <br><br> _____ |
| Story or Poem _____ <br><br> _____ <br><br> Author and/or Illustrator _____ <br><br> _____ <br><br> More Stories and/or Poems _____ <br><br> _____ <br><br> _____ | Story or Poem _____ <br><br> _____ <br><br> Author and/or Illustrator _____ <br><br> _____ <br><br> More Stories and/or Poems _____ <br><br> _____ <br><br> _____ |
| Story or Poem _____ <br><br> _____ <br><br> Author and/or Illustrator _____ <br><br> _____ <br><br> More Stories and/or Poems _____ <br><br> _____ | Story or Poem _____ <br><br> _____ <br><br> Author and/or Illustrator _____ <br><br> _____ <br><br> More Stories and/or Poems _____ <br><br> _____ |

**Name** _____**Date** _____

# Favorite Pick

Story or Poem Selected _____

Author(s) _____

Illustrator(s) _____

## Book Cover

Summary of Story or Poem: _____

_____

_____

_____

Information About Author: _____

_____

_____

_____

Information About Illustrator: _____

_____

_____

_____

**Name** _____ **Date** _____

# Sales Pitch

**Directions:** Create a full-page newspaper advertisement that will convince others to buy *The Big Book for Our Planet.*

**Name** _____ **Date** _____

# In Your Opinion

**Directions:** For each title from *The Big Book for Our Planet*, write one or two adjectives that reflects your opinion. For example, helpful, exciting, insignificant, not realistic, beautiful, fantastic, etc.

Oh World, I Wish _____

Take Time _____

The Last Days of the Giddywit _____

The Mushroom _____

Little Whale and Jonah _____

"People's Gardens" _____

Watchers _____

The Deep Green Gift _____

Wetlands _____

Pigs on Patrol _____

The Earth Game _____

Close Encounter _____

Three Cheers by Bats! _____

Why There Is Death _____

Bird _____

Prayer for Earth _____

Limericks _____

Letter from Crinkleroot _____

We Are Plooters _____

From Island to Island _____

The Boy Who Loved to Swim _____

Me and My Weeds _____

Elliot's House _____

Jellies _____

Bringing the Prairie Home _____

A Song for Francis of Assisi _____

Dear Earth _____

# 50 Simple Things Kids Can Do to Save the Earth

**Authors:** John Javna and The Earthworks Group

**Illustrator:** Michele Montez

**Publisher:** Andrews & McMeel, 1990.

**Summary:** This book demonstrates how everyone's environment is globally connected. It also provides information about how individuals can develop habits and projects that will help to save the environment. It is full of enjoyable and exciting environmentally-themed things to do.

## Pre-reading Activity

Read the book's title and then ask each student to write one thing he or she can do to save the earth. Share these ideas orally and then compile them to duplicate and distribute to the class. After reading the book, compare the students' ideas with ideas presented in the book.

## Key Concepts:

- junk food
- preserving
- acid rain
- greenhouse effect
- ozone hole
- recycle
- ground water
- insecticide
- organic
- CFC gases
- landfill
- solar energy

## Post-reading Questions

1. What is the most important thing you learned about the environment from reading this book? *(Answers may vary.)* How will what you learned help you and/or the environment? *(Answers may vary.)*

2. What changes will you make in your habits as a result of reading this book? *(Answers may vary.)*

3. What additional information do you think the author should have in this book? Why? *(Answers may vary.)*

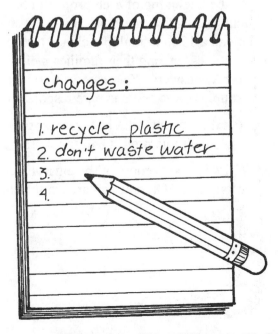

# 50 Simple Things Kids Can Do to Save the Earth *(cont.)*

## Post-reading Questions *(cont.)*

4. If you could give this book to someone as a gift, who would you give it to?  Why?  *(Answers may vary.)*

5. Why do you think the author, John Javna, and the Earthworks Group wrote a book like this?  *(Answers may vary.)*

6. Many of the activities presented in this book are enjoyable and easy to do.  Why doesn't everyone do his/her share of these activities in order to help save the Earth?  *(Answers may vary.)*

## Learning Activities

- Ask the students to bring old white or light-colored T-shirts to class.  Using fabric crayons (available in most craft stores), help the students design T-shirts that feature environmental messages about saving the Earth.

- Read the back cover of the book and then discuss forming "Environmental Patrol Clubs." Volunteer club members can patrol their neighborhoods to find things that create environmental problems.  They can then take a photograph, illustrate, or write a description of the problem. Club members can then collectively come up with solutions and attempt to implement them. (This may require help; guide students to the appropriate agency or individual who can assist them.)  Members can also keep logs of their activities.  On page 40 is an activity for making a club badge and bumper sticker.  Allow the clubs to meet for three or four weeks and then report their progress to the entire class.  Continue the clubs throughout the year, if possible.

- Write "Save the Earth" in a circle drawn on the chalkboard.  Have the students web things we can do to save the Earth.  Have them work in groups to determine what is being done in their homes or community and to add any possible solutions to the web.

- At the beginning of each project in *50 Simple Things Kids Can Do to Save the Earth* there is a multiple-choice question.  Invite the students to use these and other questions they can generate to create a 15-item multiple choice test (page 41).  Then, ask them to help create environmental awareness among their families, neighbors, and friends by administering the test and providing correct answers.  You may want to request that students record the test results and later, as a group, discuss and compare response.

- Ask the students to select and complete one of the 50 projects. Ask them to create a plan to implement this project and to report the progress or results, using page 42.

- Write to one or more of the environmentally friendly organizations on page 39, requesting free information. Organize an area in the classroom to display the materials received.

# Environmentally Friendly Organizations

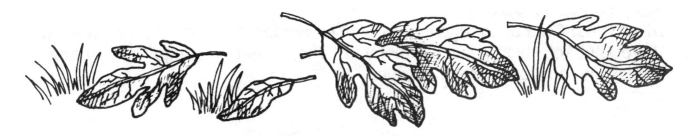

**Alliance to Save Energy**
1725 K Street, NW, Suite 914
Washington, DC  20006

**American Forestry Association**
PO Box 2000
Washington, DC  20010

**Global ReLeaf**
The American Forestry Association
PO Box 2000
Washington, DC  20013

**Greenpeace**
1611 Connecticut Avenue, NW
Washington, DC  20009

**National Arbor Day Foundation**
100 Arbor Avenue
Nebraska City, NE  68410

**National Recycling Coalition**
1101-Thirtieth Street, NW, Suite 305
Washington, DC  20007

**U.S. Environmental Protection Agency (EPA)**
401 M Street SW, A 108
Washington, DC  20060

**Center for Action on Endangered Species**
175 West Main Street
Ayer, MA  01432

**National Audubon Society**
950 Third Avenue
New York, NY  10022

**National Wildlife Federation**
1412-Sixteenth Street, NW
Washington, DC  20036

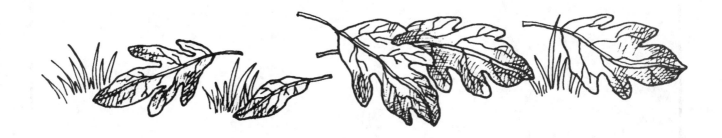

**Name** _____ **Date** _____

# Join the Club

**Directions:** Create a badge that would be appropriate for the "Environmental Patrol Club" of which you are a member. Then, create a bumper sticker that displays an environmental message.

**Name** _____ **Date** _____

# Environmental Multiple-Choice Quiz

**Directions:** Read the following questions and then select the best answer for each by circling the appropriate letter.

1. _____
    A _____ B _____ C _____

2. _____
    A _____ B _____ C _____

3. _____
    A _____ B _____ C _____

4. _____
    A _____ B _____ C _____

5. _____
    A _____ B _____ C _____

6. _____
    A _____ B _____ C _____

7. _____
    A _____ B _____ C _____

8. _____
    A _____ B _____ C _____

9. _____
    A _____ B _____ C _____

10. _____
    A _____ B _____ C _____

11. _____
    A _____ B _____ C _____

12. _____
    A _____ B _____ C _____

13. _____
    A _____ B _____ C _____

14. _____
    A _____ B _____ C _____

15. _____
    A _____ B _____ C _____

**Name** _____**Date** _____

# Project: Save the Planet

**Directions:** Select a project from *50 Simple Things Kids Can Do to Save the Earth* and complete the requested information.

**Describe the project you selected:** _____

_____

_____

_____

_____

**Plan for implementing the project:** _____

_____

_____

_____

_____

_____

**Progress or results of project:** _____

_____

_____

_____

_____

# Pollution

# *Oil Spill*

**Author:** Melvin Berger

**Illustrator:** Paul Mirocha

**Publisher:** Harper Collins Children's Books, 1994.

**Summary:** This book describes the oil spill from the tanker *Exxon Valdez* in Prince William Sound in Alaska and the damage that resulted. It explains how oil spills happen, how they can be cleaned up, and what we can do to help prevent them.

## Pre-reading Activity

Ask the children if they have heard about large oil spills into the ocean. What is the biggest one they know about? Tell students the spill from the *Exxon Valdez* was one of the biggest ever in the United States.

## Key Concepts:

- crude oil
- chemicals
- skimmer
- tanker
- poisonous
- million
- bacteria
- boom
- oil terminal
- fumes

## Post-reading Questions

1. Where did the oil spill from the tanker *Exxon Valdez* happen? *(It happened in Prince William Sound, which is a large inlet on the south coast of Alaska.)*

2. What happened to the wildlife in that area as a result of the oil spill? *(Crude oil is poisonous to fish, birds, and other animals. When they are caught in it and have to swallow it, it can kill them. Also, it coats the feathers of birds, making them unable to fly so they can't get food. Hundreds of thousands of animals died.)*

Alaska

# *Oil Spill* *(cont.)*

## Post-reading Questions *(cont.)*

3.  What are some of the ways oil spills can happen? *(tanker accidents, spills while loading and unloading tankers, leaks from undersea oil wells, storage tanks or pipelines breaking at the shore)*

4.  What are some of the ways used to clean up the spill? *(First, contain the spill by putting booms around it. Skimmers may be used to suck up the oil, pads that are like sponges can be used to soak up the oil, the oil may burned off, "oil eating" bacteria may be spread on the oil, or chemicals may be spread on the oil to make it easier to clean up.)*

5.  What are some of the ways we can help to prevent oil spills? *(Cut down on our use of oil so there will be fewer tankers. To do this, we need to use less electricity and gasoline. Also, we should find and use oil within the continental United States so oil need not be shipped. We can also tell Congress that they should put greater restrictions on tankers, such as requiring double hulls and up-to-date navigational equipment. Finally, clean-up equipment should be kept ready at key points all around the world.)*

## Learning Activities

*   Remind students that an oil spill of some type occurs almost every day somewhere in the world. Ask them to think about the book and to identify ways in which oil spill accidents occur. Make a list of the ways in which they occur. Then ask students to generate suggestions for how oil spills can be prevented.

*   One of the best ways to prevent oil spills is to use less oil. Some of the major uses of oil are fuel, heating and cooling houses and other buildings, and the automobile. Direct students to answer the questions on page 47 about the amount of oil their families consume every week.

*   An overview of the sources of energy in the United States is provided on page 48. Answer the questions on the sheet in order to complete the diagram on page 49.

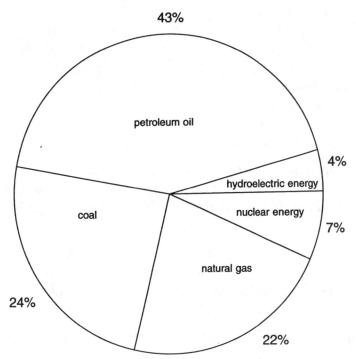

# *Oil Spill* (cont.)

## Learning Activities (cont.)

• Oil spills pollute the water and endanger animals and plants that live nearby. Write to one of the following environmental agencies and obtain information about the way in which they contribute to the prevention of oil spills. Students can work in pairs or small groups and then share the information that they obtain.

---

**Clean Water Action Project**
733 Fifteenth Street, NW
Suite 110
Washington, DC 20005

**Conservation and Renewable Energy
Inquiry and Referral Service**
PO Box 8900
Silver Springs, MD 20907

**Energy Conservation Coalition**
1525 New Hampshire Ave., NW
Washington, DC 20036

**Energy Federation Incorporated**
354 Waverly Street
Framingham, MA 01701

**Water Pollution Control Federation**
601 Wythe St.
Alexandria, VA 22314-1994

**The Oceanic Society**
1536 Sixteenth Street NW
Washington, DC 20036

---

• Ask students to work in small groups and write a children's book about oil spills. Tell them that it should be written so that children in kindergarten or first grade will understand it. After the books are completed, give students an opportunity to go to the kindergarten and first grade classrooms to read their stories and ask questions. Students can practice with each other beforehand.

• Give students an opportunity to write a story about an imaginary animal, fish, or bird that has been affected by the oil spill. Let them tell the story from the perspective of the animal, fish, or bird. Share several of the stories with the students and display them in a prominent place in the classroom.

• Ask students to work in small groups and to research one of the major leading oil spills. They should provide information about how the oil spill occurred, where it occurred, and if there were ways it could have been prevented. Also ask students to find out information about how much damage was done and how the oil was cleaned up.

• Facts about oil spills are provided on page 50; direct students to use them to answer questions.

**Name** _____**Date**_____

# Gobbling Up Oil

**Directions:** Interview anyone in your household who drives in order to answer the following questions about family oil use.

1. How many cars does your family have?

   _____

2. Ask each member of the family who drives how many gallons (liters) of gas he/she uses each week and write the answers here.

   _____

3. Add up the total gallons (liters) of gasoline used each week for all of the cars in your household.

   _____

4. Since there are 52 weeks in a year, multiply the total number of gallons (liters) of gasoline your family uses by 52 to find out how many gallons (liters) your family uses per year.

   _____

5. Now divide the total gallons (liters) of gasoline your family uses a year by the number of people in your family who ride in or use the cars. Be sure to include yourself. How many gallons (liters) per person does your family use in a year?

   _____

6. Now compare your answers to these questions with the answers of the other students in the class. What did you discover? Write down ways in which you can reduce the amount of gasoline your family uses. Talk to your family members about it and see if you can obtain their cooperation in reducing oil consumption.

   _____

   _____

   _____

   _____

**Name** _____**Date**_____

# Where Does Energy Come From?

**Directions:** Use the information that follows to label the pie chart on page 49. Draw a picture to represent your answer on the back of this page.

A. On the diagram, show that the largest source of energy in the U.S. is petroleum oil.

B. Now show that the smallest amount of energy is generated by hydroelectric energy.

C. Coal used to be the primary energy source in the U.S., and now it is the second. Place the word "coal" correctly on the diagram.

D. Natural gas is like coal as it accounts for a little over 1/5 of the sources of energy in the U.S. Include this information on the diagram.

E. Like hydroelectric energy, nuclear energy accounts for a small percentage of the sources of energy in the U.S. Label the diagram to show that it is the second smallest source of energy.

## Answer the following questions.

1. If natural gas were not available, what percentage of the energy sources in the U.S. would be lost?

   _____

   _____

2. Petroleum, coal, and natural gas account for what percent of the sources of energy in the U.S.?

   _____

   _____

3. If someone tells you that nuclear energy is a necessary energy source in the U.S., what will you tell them?

   _____

   _____

**Name** _____**Date**_____

# Pie Chart: Where Does Energy Come From?

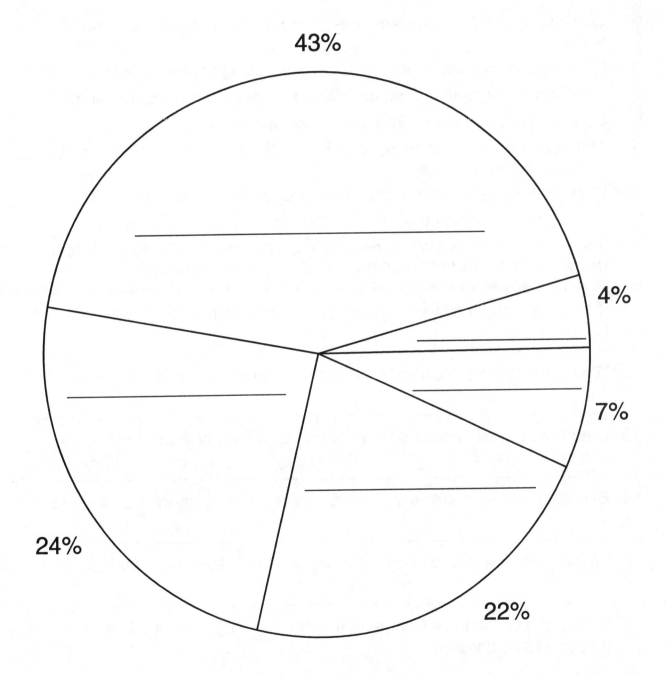

43%

4%

7%

24%

22%

**Name** _____ **Date**_____

# Killer Oil

**Directions:** Use the facts about oil spills to answer the questions that follow.

---

### Facts

- One gallon of oil can contaminate as much as five million gallons of water.
- Oil is lighter than water and slides over it, killing whatever is in its path.
- Sea animals sometimes eat oil, which kills or severely harms them.
- Oil that floats becomes more toxic over time.
- The number of tons of oil lost can be multiplied by seven to estimate the number of barrels spilled.
- Birds that eat sea life near the shore are killed.  Much plant life dies.
- The cost of cleaning up an oil spill runs into the billions of dollars.
- The oil spill in Alaska killed more than 35,000 birds.  Eighty percent of the oil spills are from human error and can be prevented.

---

1. If 100,000 tons of oil were spilled, how many barrels of oil would that be?

   _____

2. Why is more water polluted than the amount of oil that is dumped?

   _____

3. Over time the oil becomes less dangerous.  True or False?

   _____

4. Besides fish and animals in the water, what else is harmed by an oil spill?

   _____

5. Which of the facts above do you think is most disturbing?  Explain why.

   _____

6. Select one of the facts from above to teach to your family.  Identify the fact that you have chosen.

   _____

# *Recycling*

**Authors:** Joan Kalbacker and Emilie U. Lepthieu

**Publisher:** Children's Press, Inc., 1991.

**Summary:** This book illustrates how the ever-growing amount of garbage and refuse threatens the environment and how recycling can help in conservation efforts.

## Pre-reading Activity

Show the students the cover of the book and read its title. Write "recycling" on the chalkboard to create a web of their responses and ask them to name all the things they know that can be recycled. For example:

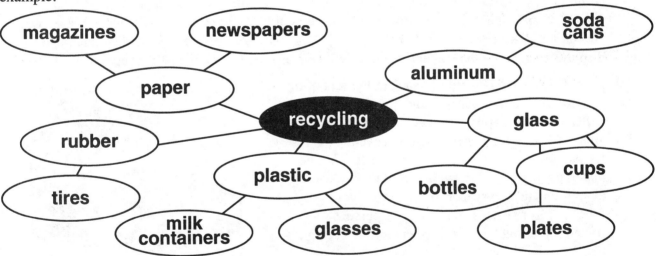

## Key Concepts:

- mulch
- landfill
- composting
- degradable
- toxic
- decompose
- incinerator
- corrugated
- resins

## Post-reading Questions

1. What will happen if Americans continue to throw away four to six pounds of garbage every day? *(There will be no place left to dump it.)* What do you think will happen then? *(Answers may vary.)*

2. The authors of *Recycling* indicated that although more than half of the garbage in North America could be recycled, only one-tenth of it actually is. What needs to be done so that more garbage is recycled? *(Answers may vary.)*

# *Recycling* (cont.)

## Post-reading Questions (cont.)

3. How can recycled newsprint be used? *(It can be used for newspaper, tagboard, note cards, insulation, animal bedding, etc.)*

4. How can you tell if you are using a product that has been made from recycled materials? *(A special symbol is included on the product.)*

5. What are some of the problems that are connected with using plastic products? *(Answers might include they are not easily, or may never be, decomposed; they pollute beaches and interfere with wildlife.)*

6. What do many people do with their used oil? *(They dump oil on the ground, pour it down sewers, etc.)* Why is this a problem? *(Used oil seeps into ground and pollutes water sources.)* What should people do with used oil? *(Take the oil where it can be recycled.)*

## Learning Activities

- Ask individuals or small groups to adopt a local area to clean up and beautify. Prior to implementation, ask students to fill out and submit the proposal found on page 53 to a "screening committee." The peer screening committee is to discuss proposals for their feasibility and to determine any safety issues involved. Proposals will be returned to students with an approval, "needs more discussion," etc. Once the project is completed, students should fill out page 54 for display. Encourage the students to compare their proposals with their final reports.

- As a class project, identify a place in the school or classroom where newspaper and aluminum can be collected. Place appropriate containers in these areas. Make arrangements with a recycling center for pickup or recruit parent volunteers to take the materials there. Most recycling centers pay for aluminum and newspaper; this can be a good way for the class to earn some money to purchase something to put back into the environment (e.g., trees).

- Ask students to collect data, using the survey on page 55. They should interview 10 people (parents, brothers, sisters, neighbors, etc.) in order to project how many pounds of garbage they think they produce per day. The students will also ask them to carry and throw all their trash into a plastic garbage bag. At the end of the 24-hour period, the collected garbage should be weighed and recorded on the survey. Tell the students to remind their subjects to include garbage produced at home for meal preparation, e.g., empty cereal boxes, milk containers, etc. Allow time for students to compare data and then to compile all the data together.

- As a follow-up to the Garbage Data Survey, invite someone from your local department of sanitation to your classroom to discuss what happens to the garbage collected. Prior to the visit, ask the students to work in small groups to prepare questions. For example, Where is our garbage taken? Do most people separate their garbage? Approximately how many pounds (tons) of garbage is collected each week? Is more garbage being collected now than five years ago? What can we do to help?

**Name** _____**Date** _____

# Clean-up and Beautification Proposal

1. Area I (we) plan to adopt _____

2. Location of adopted area _____

3. Why did you select this area to adopt? _____

_____

_____

4. Describe your plan of action for cleaning up and beautifying the area you are adopting. _____

_____

_____

5. How much time will it take? _____

6. Will it cost anything?  If yes, how much? _____

7. Current photo or illustration of the area you adopted:

**Name** _____**Date**_____

# Clean-up and Beautification Final Report

1. Area I (we) adopted _____

2. Location of area adopted _____

3. Briefly describe what you did to improve this area. _____

   _____

   _____

4. How much time did it take? _____

5. Did it cost anything?  If yes, how much? _____

6. What, if anything, is still needed for this area? _____

   _____

   _____

7. What is your plan for keeping this a clean and beautiful area? _____

   _____

   _____

8. Photo or illustration of the area after you completed your project:

**Name** _____ **Date** _____

# Garbage Data Survey

| Name | Predicted Pounds of Garbage | Actual Pounds Collected |
|---|---|---|
| 1. _____ | _____ | _____ |
| 2. _____ | _____ | _____ |
| 3. _____ | _____ | _____ |
| 4. _____ | _____ | _____ |
| 5. _____ | _____ | _____ |
| 6. _____ | _____ | _____ |
| 7. _____ | _____ | _____ |
| 8. _____ | _____ | _____ |
| 9. _____ | _____ | _____ |
| 10. _____ | _____ | _____ |
| Total_____ | _____ | _____ |

1. How many total pounds of garbage did subjects predict they would collect?

   _____

2. How many actual total pounds of garbage were collected?

   _____

3. How many actual total pounds of garbage would this be in one week?

   _____

4. How many actual total pounds of garbage would this be in one year?

   _____

5. What is done with this garbage each day?

   _____

6. Is there a way these people might cut down on their daily garbage? Explain.

   _____

7. Create a bumper sticker to motivate others to create less garbage.

# Marjory Stoneman Douglas, Voice of the Everglades

**Author:** Jennifer Bryant

**Illustrator:** Larry Raymond

**Publisher:** Twenty-First Century Books, 1992.

**Summary:** Marjory Stoneman Douglas is a living answer to the question, "What can I do to save the _____? In her case, the question can be completed with "Everglades." For more than 60 years, she led a fight to preserve and protect this unique and beautiful part of the world.

## Pre-reading Activity

Show the children the map on the frontispiece of the book. Discuss where the state of Florida is. Show them the part of Florida once covered by the Everglades and the part now covered. Point out that the Everglades might not exist at all if it were not for Mary Stoneman Douglas.

## Key Concepts:

- conservation
- ecosystem
- wildlife
- refuge

- sawgrass
- environmentalist
- swamp
- marsh

- ecology
- hurricane
- homesteader
- preservation

## Post-reading Questions

1. Do you think one person can really help save our environment? *(Yes; Marjory Stoneman Douglas is an example of someone who did.)*

2. What are the Everglades like? *(The Everglades are a huge area of shallow, slow-moving water where mostly sawgrass grows, interspersed with islands with trees inhabited by many animals, including alligators and Florida panthers and many, many birds. Marjory Stoneman Douglas calls it "a river of grass.")*

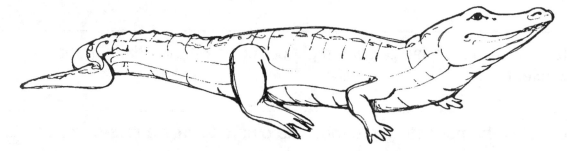

# *Marjory Stoneman Douglas, Voice of the Everglades* (cont.)

## Post-reading Questions *(cont.)*

3. What did she realize about the Everglades that no one else ever had? *(She noticed that the Everglades were a unique system of interdependent parts like a living thing that could be killed by destroying one of its vital parts; that is, it is an ecosystem.)*

4. Why do you think the government encouraged the building of dams and canals in the Everglades? *(to control the flooding of the land so it could be used by farmers, ranchers, and home builders)*

5. What do you feel are some of the greatest accomplishments of Marjory Stoneman Douglas' crusade? *(the establishment of part of the area of the Everglades as a National Park in 1947; halting the building of a huge airport in the Everglades; legislation requiring the clean up of the Everglades)*

6. Do you think you would like to know Marjory Stoneman Douglas? What would you ask her if you met her? *(Answers may vary.)*

7. What does Marjory Stoneman Douglas mean when she says, "The children are our whole future"? *(She is happy that so many children are now able to take part in educational environmental programs. Perhaps she feels that in the future, when they have grown, children will take better care of our environment.)*

## Learning Activities

- Florida became a state in 1845, and the idea of draining the Everglades was immediately promoted. Have students give several arguing points for (the developers) and against (the environmentalists) draining the Everglades. Each group should list four points they would like the legislature to consider.

- Use the glossary words in the box on Everglades Vocabulary to complete the sentences on page 60.

- Ask students to find and share library books on or by Marjory Stoneman Douglas, such as *The Everglades: River of Grass.*

- Identify rivers and streams in your area. Determine the extent to which your local streams, ponds, rivers, and lakes need help because they are polluted. What are some ways you can tell they are in trouble? Is there trash along the banks or flowing in the water? Is the water filled with broken branches and leaves? How much garbage is around the river or floating in it? Is the river sudsy or discolored? Has the body of water changed shape dramatically? For example, is it wider or deeper than it once was? Is there any runoff from factories or nearby areas that is polluting the water?

# *Marjory Stoneman Douglas, Voice of the Everglades* *(cont.)*

## Learning Activities *(cont.)*

- Ask students to complete the word search on page 61 of birds and animals that live in the Everglades.

- On page 62, complete the math word problems related to Marjory Stoneman Douglas and the Everglades.

- There are many organizations that are concerned about water pollution and the wetlands. These organizations promote and encourage conservation. Form students into teams of three and assign each an organization to contact as follows:

    - Write to the organization to find out what its purpose and policies are.

    - Summarize what they learn on a chart and present an oral report.

    - Make a display of materials that they receive.

**The National Water Alliance**
1225 I Street, NW, Suite 300
Washington, DC 20005

**National Coalition for Marine Conservation**
PO Box 23298
Savannah, GA 31403

**National Oceanic and Atmospheric Administration**
Office of Public Affairs
United States Department of Commerce
Washington, DC 20230

**National Wetlands Technical Council**
3616 P Street, NW
Suite 200
Washington, DC 20036

**North American Lake Management Society**
100 Connecticut Avenue, NW
Suite 202
Washington, DC 20036

**Seacoast Antipollution League**
5 Market Street
Portsmouth, NH 03801

**Soil and Water Conservation Society**
7515 NE Ankeny Road
Ankeny, IA 50021

**Water Pollution Control Federation**
601 Wythe Street
Alexandria, VA 22314-1994

**National Water Center**
PO Box 548
Eureka Springs, AR 72632

**New York Sea Grant Institute**
37 Elk Street
New York, NY 12246

Name _____ Date_____

# Draining the Everglades: For and Against

**Directions:** Identify four points that developers might make to encourage people to drain the Everglades.  Then, identify four points environmentalists might make to prevent them from doing so.

### Developers

1. _____

_____

2. _____

_____

3. _____

_____

4. _____

_____

### Environmentalists

1. _____

_____

2. _____

_____

3. _____

_____

4. _____

_____

**Name** _____ **Date** _____

# Everglades Vocabulary

**Directions:** Select words from the vocabulary box below to complete the sentences that follow. You may find that you do not use all of the words. Write your own last sentence and provide the correct vocabulary word from the box.

| | | |
|---|---|---|
| conservation | Okeechobee Lake | pollution |
| Marjory Stoneman Douglas | Everglades | poacher |
| | ecology | pesticide |
| river of grass | swamp | hurricane |
| canal | sawgrass | homesteader |
| Florida | preservation | |

1. A type of grass of sedge with tough, sharp edges that grows in the Everglades area is _____ .

2. The process by which an environment is kept preserved in its natural condition is _____ .

3. A person who kills animals illegally is a _____ .

4. A severe tropical storm with strong winds and heavy rains is the/a _____ .

5. A waterway dug across land is a _____ .

6. A vast, shallow, slow-moving river in South Florida is the _____ .

7. The study of things living in their environment is _____ .

8. A person who makes a home in a newly settled place is a _____ .

9. A woman who influenced the history of the Everglades is _____ .

10. _____

    _____

**Name** _____ **Date** _____

# Everglades Word Search

**Directions:** Find and circle the names of the birds and animals that live in the Everglades in the puzzle below.

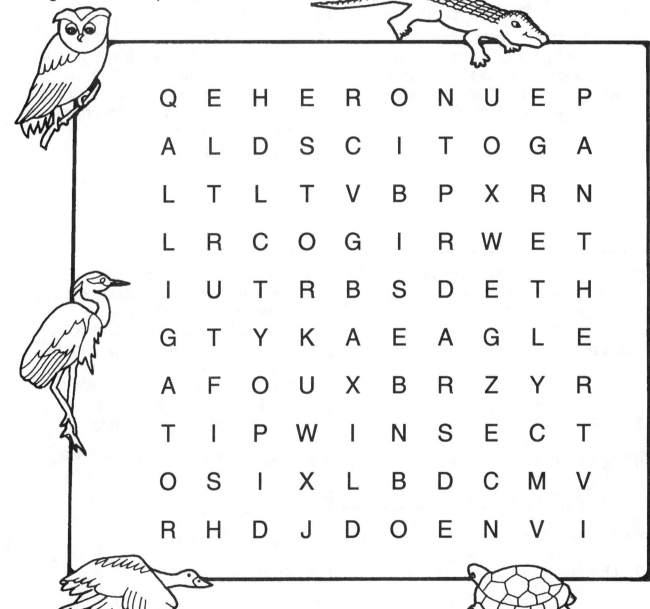

```
Q E H E R O N U E P
A L D S C I T O G A
L T L T V B P X R N
L R C O G I R W E T
I U T R B S D E T H
G T Y K A E A G L E
A F O U X B R Z Y R
T I P W I N S E C T
O S I X L B D C M V
R H D J D O E N V I
```

| | | | |
|---|---|---|---|
| ALLIGATOR | CRAB | EAGLE | EGRET |
| FISH | HERON | IBIS | INSECT |
| OWL | PANTHER | STORK | TURTLE |

**Name** _____ **Date** _____

# Everglades Math

Directions: Complete the following word problems.  Make up your own word problem using information about Marjory Stoneman Douglas and the Everglades for problem 5.  Be sure to provide the answer.

---

① Marjory Stoneman Douglas' book, *The Everglades: The River of Grass*, was first published in 1948.  How many years ago was that?

Answer:

② The Everglades was originally a 4,000 square mile area.  Since then, the Everglades has shrunk by 1/5 so that it is now only 80% of the size it once was.  What square-mile area does the Everglades now cover?

Answer:

③ In 1915, Marjory Stoneman Douglas was 25 years old.  In what year was she born?

Answer:

④ When Marjory Stoneman Douglas first visited the Everglades, she would see as many as 40,000 birds flying overhead in one swoop.  Over time, birds visited the Everglades in much smaller numbers  until she saw only about 4,000 birds at a time.  What is the difference between the amount she first saw and what she saw later?

Answer:

⑤

Answer:

---

# *Come Back, Salmon*

**Author:** Molly Cone

**Photographer:** Sidnee Wheelwrigh

**Publisher:** The Sierra Club, 1992.

**Summary:** *Come Back, Salmon* describes how the Jackson Elementary School in Everett, Washington, cleaned up a nearby stream, stocked it with salmon, and preserved it as an unpolluted place where salmon could return to spawn. The book also contains beautiful photographs.

## Pre-reading Activity

Show the students the cover of the book and read its title. Duplicate the Literature Log on page 65 and ask the students to complete the "before reading" section. Allow time to discuss their answers. Then, after reading the story, ask the students to complete the "after reading" section of the Literature Log on their own and to share their responses in small groups.

## Key Concepts:

- watershed
- smolts
- parr marks
- alevins
- embryo
- spawn
- melt
- fry
- yolk sac
- redd
- silt
- eyed egg

## Post-reading Questions

1. What is the prime source of every stream? (*its watershed*) Explain how the watershed can effect life in the stream. (*Answers might include that any contamination such as spilling oil or paint thinner, if enough people do it, can contaminate fish and plant life in the stream*).

2. What did the students of Jackson Elementary School do to "bring back" Pigeon Creek? (*Answers might include they worked together to pick up many truckloads of garbage.*) How did some of the nearby residents feel about this project? (*The students were wasting their time.*)

3. What did the students have to do to keep people from continuing to dump garbage? (*They patrolled creek banks after school and on weekends.*) What do you think about this? (*Answers may vary.*)

# *Come Back, Salmon* (cont.)

## Post-reading Questions (cont.)

4. When a salmon approaches maturity, what does it do? (*It swims back to its original home.*) How does it know to do this? (*Every salmon is born with this instinct.*)

5. Only one or two salmon out of a hundred complete the entire journey from stream (place of birth) to ocean and back again. What happens to the remaining salmon? (*Answers might include that many water birds, as well as whales, seals, and sea lions, feed on salmon. Also, many salmon are caught for human consumption*).

6. How do you think the students felt when they put the fish they had raised into Pigeon Creek and said goodbye? (*Answers may vary.*)

## Learning Activities

- Ask the students to recall the stages of the salmon from the eyed egg to an alevin by completing page 66.

- Write the following sentence on the chalkboard: "To accomplish anything, you have to have a dream. Everything worthwhile starts with a dream." Remind your students that Mr. King told his class this when others told them they were wasting their time cleaning up Pigeon Creek. Ask the students to write a brief reaction to the statement in their journals and then allow time to share.

- Reinforce the key concepts of this book by assigning the students the crossword puzzle on page 67.

- Tell the students to use the cinquain poetry form on page 68 to write a poem about something related to the life of a salmon or the Jackson Elementary School project and then to illustrate it.

- Ask the students to complete the Salmon Information Frame on page 69. After they have completed the frame, divide them into small groups to discuss and debate their responses.

- There is available a piece of software, "Puddles to Pondwater," that invites students to observe, study, and protect freshwater creatures around the world. For more information, contact NIAD Corp. (905) 470-0868; fax (905) 513-8179. This software would provide a good follow-up to *Come Back, Salmon.*

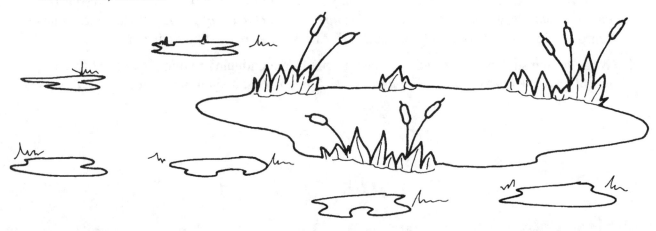

**Name** _____ **Date** _____

# Literature Log

Title of Book _____

Author _____

Illustrator/Photographer _____

**Directions:** Complete the "Before Reading" section before listening to *Come Back, Salmon.* After hearing the book, complete the "After Reading" section.

**Before Reading**

1. Why might you be interested in reading this book? _____

_____

2. What do you already know about this topic? _____

_____

3. What are some questions you would like to ask before reading the story? _____

_____

4. What do you think the book is about? _____

_____

**After Reading**

1. Why did the author write this book? _____

_____

2. Are you satisfied with this story? Why or why not? _____

_____

3. Would you want to read this story again? _____

_____

4. What questions do you still need answers to? _____

_____

5. What is the outstanding feature of this book? _____

_____

**Name** _____ **Date** _____

# Salmon Development

**Directions:** Identify the order in which salmon develop from an eyed egg to an alevin by numbering the illustrations A–F from numbers 1–6. Write a short sentence or phrase below each picture to describe what is occurring.

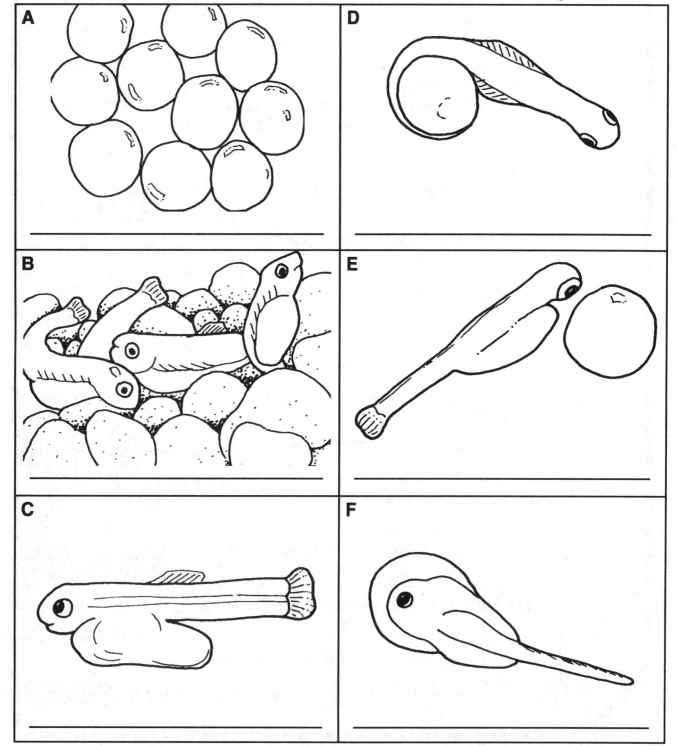

A

D

B

E

C

F

**Name** _____**Date** _____

# Salmon Crossword

**Directions:** Use the clues to complete the crossword puzzle.

**Down**

1. Draining area around a stream or river

4. Soft dirt in bottom of stream

7. Dark bars on the sides of the fry

9. Sperm-filled fluid sprayed by a male fish to fertilize eggs

**Across**

2. Newly hatched salmon with its yolk sac still attached

3. Food supply attached to baby salmon when it hatches

5. To lay eggs or fertilize them

6. A month-old salmon egg at the stage when the embryo is large and dark eyes can be seen through egg membrane

8. Baby salmon that have used up their yolk sacs and are ready to find their own food

10. Young salmon that are ready to migrate to ocean

11. Hole in bottom of stream in which a female salmon lays her eggs

12. Tiny living thing inside a fertilized egg

**Name** _____ **Date** _____

# Salmon Cinquain

**Directions:** Write a cinquain related to *Come Back, Salmon,* using the guidelines that follow. Illustrate your poem in the area below.

Line 1: one-word title                                     **Salmon**

Line 2: two words describing the title          **sparkling, spotted**

Line 3: three words relating an action          **flashing in water**

Line 4: four words conveying a feeling          **I enjoy your swimming**

Line 5: one word referring to the title          **Fish**

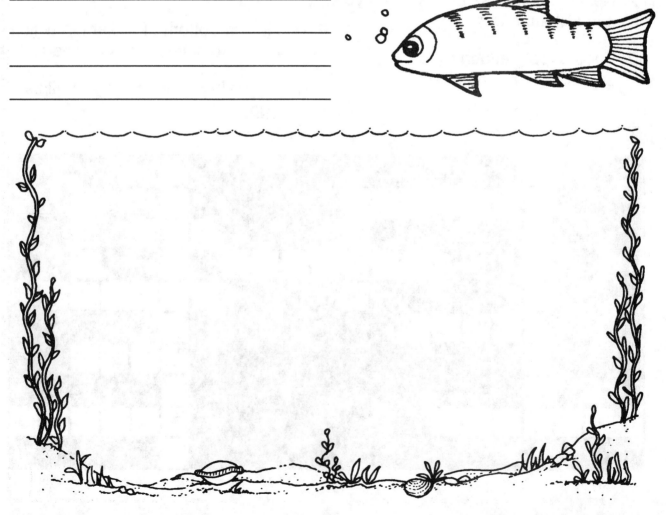

**Name** _____ **Date** _____

# Salmon Information Frame

**Directions:** After listening to *Come Back, Salmon,* complete the following "Information Frame."

This story was written to teach us about_____

_____

_____.

One important fact I learned was _____

_____

_____.

Another fact I learned was _____

_____

_____.

A third important fact I learned was_____

_____

_____.

If I were to remember one important thing from this story, it would be_____

_____.

because _____.

I (circle one) would/would not recommend this book for a friend to read
because _____

_____

_____.

# *Recycle!*

**Author:** Gail Gibbons

**Publisher:** Little, Brown & Co, 1992.

**Summary:** This book explains the process of recycling from start to finish. It discusses what happens to glass, paper, plastic, and aluminum cans when they are recycled into new products.

## Pre-reading Activity

Introduce *Recycle!* by asking the students what the word "recycle" means to them and how recycling affects their lives.

## Key Concepts:

- biodegradable
- deposit
- sterilized
- bauxite

- polymers
- polystyrene
- ozone layer
- chlorofluorocarbons

- silica
- landfills
- leachate

## Post-reading Questions

1. Why don't people like having landfills near where they live? *(Answers might include that landfills might smell and that some of the leachate might leak into the soil and drinking water.)*

2. Why does it take less energy and create less pollution to make new glass from old glass? *(Answers might include that recycling means that fresh sand, lime, and soda ash will not have to be used.)*

3. Why are you told not to buy or use polystyrene products? *(Answers might include it is not biodegradable and there are few useful products that can be made from recycled polystyrene.)*

4. What is the most important point you learned from reading this book? *(Answers may vary.)*

5. If you could add information to this book, what would it be? *(Answers may vary.)*

6. What things do you and your family do to help with recycling? *(Answers may vary.)*

# Recycle! *(cont.)*

## Learning Activities

- Ask students to assist you in identifying other books written by Gail Gibbons, as well as other books by different authors that are all about recycling and related topics (page 72). Create a display of these books.

- Ask the students to complete the true or false worksheet (page 73).

- Read and discuss each of the "What You Can Do" suggestions on the last page of *Recycle!* Then, ask the students to think of additional things they and their families can do to control amounts of accumulated garbage and trash and list them on page 74.

- Divide the students into small groups to create large posters encouraging people to be involved in recycling. Display the posters around the school.

- Collect a variety of what would be considered trash or garbage, such as plastic meat and vegetable trays, plastic rings from cans, Styrofoam packaging chips, etc. Tell the students to create a piece of art (sculpture, collage, etc.) from the trash and garbage. Display the students' work.

- On page 80 there is a drawing of "Mt. Trashmore," a dump. Have students draw items that might be found there and indicate which ones could be recycled.

- Help the students create a "Trivial Pursuit" game, using facts from "Can You Believe . . . ?" at the end of *Recycle!* Have them add facts they find in other resource materials.

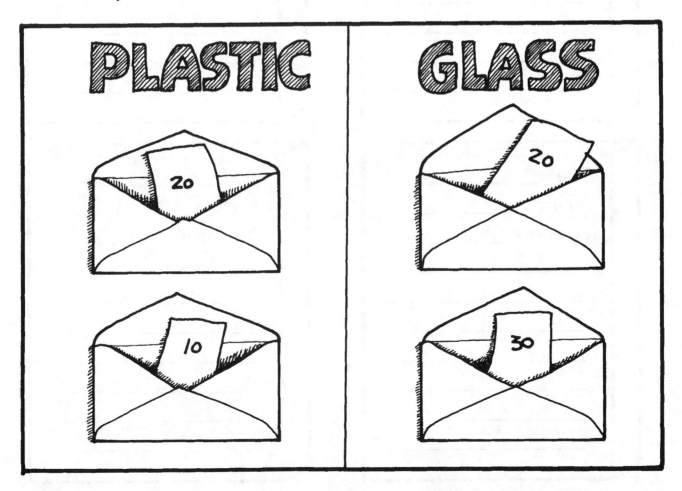

**Name** _____ **Date** _____

# More Books by Gail Gibbons

**Directions:** Now that you have read *Recycle!* by Gail Gibbons, you might be interested in reading some of the other more than fifty titles she has written  or reading more books about recycling and other environmentally-related topics. Read several books and then complete the following.

Title _____

Author _____

Summary _____

_____

_____

_____

_____

_____

_____

Title _____

Author _____

Summary _____

_____

_____

_____

_____

_____

_____

Title _____

Author _____

Summary _____

_____

_____

_____

_____

_____

Title _____

Author _____

Summary _____

_____

_____

_____

_____

_____

**Name** _____**Date** _____

# Recycling: True or False

**Directions:** Read the following statements and write either true or false next to each one.

_____ 1. Glass bottles biodegrade very quickly.

_____ 2. Creating a landfill for garbage is one solution to the vast amounts of garbage being collected today.

_____ 3. Another name for polystyrene is Styrofoam.

_____ 4. It costs more money to make new polystyrene than to recycle it.

_____ 5. Recycling paper helps to save trees and forests.

_____ 6. Plastic cannot be recycled and used again.

_____ 7. Recycling helps to save natural resources.

_____ 8. All glass bottles can be returned for a deposit.

_____ 9. Environmentalists believe we should buy more polystyrene products.

_____ 10. Recycling can help make our planet a safe and healthier place to live.

Write four additional true or false statements related to *Recycle!* by Gail Gibbons. Ask a friend to answer them.

_____ 1. _____

_____

_____ 2. _____

_____

_____ 3. _____

_____

_____ 4. _____

_____

**Name** _____**Date** _____

# Ideas for Recycling

**Directions:** Discuss recycling with your family and decide upon several solutions to reducing waste.  Illustrate each idea.

| Idea | Illustration | Idea | Illustration |
|------|-------------|------|-------------|
| Idea | Illustration | Idea | Illustration |
| Idea | Illustration | Idea | Illustration |
| Idea | Illustration | Idea | Illustration |

# Cartons, Cans, and Orange Peels: Where Does Your Garbage Go?

**Author:** Joanna Foster

**Publisher:** Clarion Books, 1991.

**Summary:** This book discusses the makeup of trash and garbage and the various methods of disposing of it. The author emphasizes recycling as an option for creating less garbage.

## Pre-reading Activity

Show the students the cover of the book and read the title. Then, read the chapter titles in the table of contents. Ask the students which chapters they are most interested in and why.

## Key Concepts:

- baghouse
- hazardous waste
- biodegradable
- contaminate
- leachate
- sludge
- methane
- solid waste
- bulky waste
- white goods
- landfill

## Post-reading Questions

1. Do you think *Cartons, Cans, and Orange Peels: Where Does You Garbage Go?* is a good title for this book? Why or why not? *(Answers may vary.)*

2. What do you perceive as the best way to reduce the amount of garbage being produced today? *(Answers may vary.)*

3. What is the difference between garbage and trash? *(Garbage is waste food, and trash is waste that is not food.)*

4. Collecting garbage costs a lot of money. What one thing did the author say costs taxpayers more money? *(funding schools)*

5. Why are few open dumps being used today? *(Answers might include that dumps smell, are ugly, and may be hazardous to people's health.)* What is being done instead? *(Most towns are burning trash.)*

6. What is the most important piece of information you learned from reading this book? *(Answers may vary.)*

# *Cartons, Cans, and Orange Peels: Where Does Your Garbage Go?* *(cont.)*

## Learning Activities

- As a class project, use page 77 to develop a one-month environmental calendar. Send copies of the completed calendar home with the students. Each day allow students time to share their progress with the activities.

- If possible, arrange a class visit to a recycling center in your community. If this is not possible, obtain more information from books and other sources such as the National Recycling Coalition, 1101 - Thirtieth Street, NW, Suite 305, Washington, DC 20007. Then, as a class project, set up a recycling program for your school or community. You can receive a helpful, free, step-by-step guide for setting up a recycling program by contacting United States Conference of Mayors, 1620 I Street, NW, Washington, DC 20006 (202) 293-7330. You may also want the class to create editorials for the newspaper, posters, bumper stickers, flyers, etc.

- Ask the students to complete the "before listening" section of page 78 before reading *Cartons, Cans, and Orange Peels: Where Does Your Garbage Go?* Divide students into small groups to discuss their responses. After students listen to the book, ask them to complete the after listening section. Allow the groups time to meet again to discuss their new responses.

- Invite someone from the local department of sanitation to your class to discuss how garbage is handled in your community. As a class, prepare questions prior to the visit. For example, how many tons of garbage are collected each week in your community? What happens to the garbage? Are people recycling? Is the amount of garbage produced increasing or decreasing? How long will we be able to dispose of garbage in the same manner as we are today? Finally, ask the visitor what you as a class can do to help this process.

- Many communities encourage trash sorting so that materials can be recycled easily. Post the graph on page 79 on a bulletin board. Then, ask the students to fill in their names on the graph if they and their families sort and/or recycle any of these items. Discuss the results.

**Name** _____ **Date** _____

# Calendar of Recycling Activities

**Directions:** Write the name of the month and appropriate numerals on the calendar. Then, fill in empty blocks with environmental projects related to trash and garbage.

**Month:** _____

| SUNDAY | MONDAY | TUESDAY | WEDNESDAY | THURSDAY | FRIDAY | SATURDAY |
|---|---|---|---|---|---|---|
| Do not use anything made of plastic or Styrofoam. | | Find a place where you can keep a box for collecting glass. | | | | |
| | Give old books you no longer want to a local library or hospital. | | | | Find a place where you can keep a box for collecting aluminum cans. | |
| | | | Start a compost pile. | | | Keep a plastic or paper bag to use again. |
| | Find a toy you are about to throw away and give it to someone who can use it. | | | | Find something in your garbage that you could use. For example, use a clean can for a pencil holder. | |
| | | | Pick up a piece or two of trash that someone else has littered. | | | |

**Name** _____**Date** _____

# Test Your Knowledge

**Directions:** Before listening to the book *Cartons, Cans, and Orange Peels: Where Does Your Garbage Go?*, read the following sentences. If you think the sentence is correct, write "yes" in the "Before" column and "no" if you think the sentence is incorrect. After listening to the book, read the sentences again and mark them in the same way, using the "After" column.

Before        After

_____    _____    1. Landfills are a safe place to dispose of garbage.

_____    _____    2. A paper napkin would be considered biodegradable.

_____    _____    3. Yard waste can become part of a compost pile.

_____    _____    4. Burning garbage is a good alternative to burying it.

_____    _____    5. Many materials such as aluminum cans can be recycled over and over again.

_____    _____    6. Only aluminum is good for recycling.

_____    _____    7. Glass must be separated by color in order to be recycled.

_____    _____    8. It takes about seventeen trees to make one ton of paper.

_____    _____    9. Batteries, insect spray, etc., should not be thrown in with regular garbage.

_____    _____    10. Many people throughout the USA throw their garbage into open dumps.

**Name** _____ **Date**_____

# Recycling Graph

**Directions:** Please write your name in the column under any of the items that you and your family recycle.

| Newspapers | Glass | Aluminum Cans | Plastics |
|---|---|---|---|
|  |  |  |  |
|  |  |  |  |
|  |  |  |  |
|  |  |  |  |
|  |  |  |  |
|  |  |  |  |
|  |  |  |  |
|  |  |  |  |
|  |  |  |  |
|  |  |  |  |
|  |  |  |  |
|  |  |  |  |

Name _____ Date_____

# Mt. Trashmore

**Directions:** Here is an outline of Mt. Trashmore, a dump. Add additional items that might be found at this dump. Then, circle the items that could be recycled.

# Endangered Species

# *Dolphin!*

**Author:** June Behrens

**Publisher:** Children's Press, 1989.

**Summary:** This book describes and illustrates the many types of dolphins in the world, points out how they have interacted with humans since ancient history, and provides many stories of how they have aided humans in danger.

## Pre-reading Activity

Show the children the picture of the good-natured dolphin on the cover of the book. Have they ever seen a dolphin? Have they ever watched *Flipper* on TV?

## Key Concepts:

- mammal
- dorsal fin
- Pelorus Jack
- pod
- cortex
- echolocation
- acrobat
- oceanarium
- Delphinidae

## Post-reading Questions

1. Are dolphins related to whales? *(Yes, they are, but they are smaller. Sometimes they are called "small-toothed whales.")*

2. What kind of dolphin was Flipper? What do you know about that type of dolphin? *(Flipper was a bottle-nosed dolphin. Bottle-nosed dolphins are easy to find and can be trained. They are the ones you usually see in marine shows.)*

3. What other kinds of dolphins did you read about? *(Pacific white-sided dolphins, Risso's dolphin, spinner dolphins, spotted dolphins, common dolphins, Southern and Northern right-whale dolphins, and river dolphins)*

# *Dolphin!* *(cont.)*

## Post-reading Questions *(cont.)*

4. How do we know dolphins are intelligent? *(Answers may vary but might include that they learn quickly, they seem to like to perform, they make up games, and often they try to help people in trouble in the water.)*

5. Sometimes tuna boats accidentally catch dolphins with the tuna in their nets, and the dolphins drown. What have people done to make tuna fishing safer for the dolphins? *(They have threatened not to buy any cans of tuna from companies that don't protect the dolphins.)*

6. What would you say to someone you thought was going to hurt a dolphin? *(Answers may vary.)*

7. Which one is your favorite story of dolphins helping humans? *(Answers may vary.)*

## Learning Activities

- Design a tuna can that will inform purchasers that the tuna has been caught in nets that do not attract dolphins and kill them (page 85).

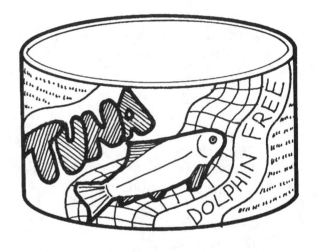

- Dolphins travel through the water at speeds of 25 miles an hour. If humans are in top condition, they can run approximately 6 miles an hour. Look up the travel speed of other mammals and make a list of their names and their travel speeds.

- Ask the students why dolphins are referred to as small-toothed whales. Then, compare and contrast characteristics of dolphins and whales.

- There are many types of dolphins, including the bottled-nosed dolphin, Commerson's dolphin, spinner dolphin, spotted dolphin, Risso's dolphin, and Pacific white-sided dolphin. Ask students to write a brief report on each type of dolphin. In what ways are they the same and different?

- Page 86 provides some vocabulary words related to dolphins and their descriptions. Tell the students to select the correct word from the box and write it next to the appropriate description.

- Page 87 provides a conversation in "dolphin talk" between a mother and baby; ask the students to translate it. Remember, the students get to make up this conversation since we don't yet know how to translate dolphin talk.

# *Dolphin!* *(cont.)*

## Learning Activities *(cont.)*

- Tell students the Greek story of Arion, a musician who sailed from Italy to Greece after winning a music competition. Explain to students how a herd of dolphins was attracted to Arion after he played a tune and how they saved him. Find a book on Arion and read it to the students.

- Tell students that until 60 million years ago, what are now whales and dolphins lived on land. The reason they returned to the sea was to find food. Follow the directions on page 88 to find out more.

- Page 90 provides students with an opportunity to be "interviewed on television" to provide important information about protecting dolphins.

- As you know, dolphins live in oceans. On page 89, information about oceans is provided along with questions. Ask students to complete the sheet.

- Inform students that there are many organizations established to help protect the dolphin. Provide the names of these organizations and ask students to work in small groups and write a letter to each of the organizations to obtain information about what they can do to help save the dolphin.

**Cousteau Society**
425 E. 52nd St.
New York, NY 10022

**Sierra Club**
730 Polk St.
San Francisco, CA 94109

**Greenpeace**
427 Bloor St. West
Toronto, Ontario M5S 1X7 Canada

**Worldwide Fund for Nature**
60 St. Claire Ave., E. Suite 201
Toronto, Ontario M4T 1N5 Canada

**National Oceanic and Atmospheric Administration**
Office of Public Affairs
United States Department of Commerce
Washington, DC 20230

**National Coalition for Marine Conservation**
PO Box 23298
Savannah, GA 31403

**Name** _____ **Date**_____

# Dolphin-Free Tuna

**Directions:** Design a label for a tuna can that will provide information to shoppers that the tuna was caught without harm to dolphins.

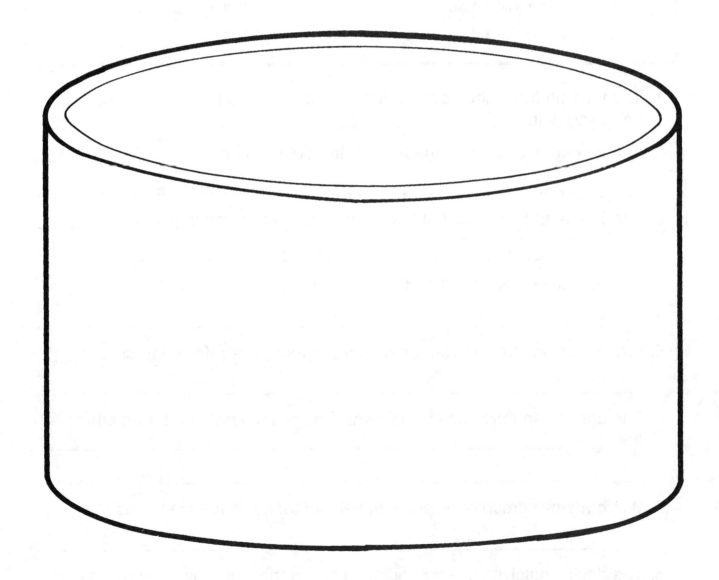

**Name** _____**Date**_____

# Dolphin Vocabulary

**Directions:** Use the vocabulary in the box below to complete the sentences that follow.

| | |
|---|---|
| • dorsal fin | • fluke |
| • sonar | • flipper |
| • blowhole | • herd |
| • nostril | • pod |

1. The hole on top of the head of dolphins and whales that they use for breathing is the _____.

2. The fin that is on or near the back of the dolphin is the _____ _____.

3. The broad and flat limb that the dolphin uses for swimming is a _____ _____.

4. The flat tail of a dolphin that it also uses to swim is a_____ _____.

5. When dolphins travel together in a large group, it is referred to as a _____ _____.

6. The opening in the head through which dolphins obtain air for breathing is the _____ _____.

7. When a small group of dolphins travel together, it is referred to as a_____ _____.

8. The device dolphins use for finding things in the water by reflecting sound waves is _____.

**Name** _____**Date**_____

# Dolphin Talk

**Directions:** As an animal researcher, you have been asked to translate a conversation between a mother dolphin and her baby.

**Mother Dolphin:** Squeak ekk aoa eh, eek eerk squeak.

**Baby Dolphin:**   Squeak, squeak! Eek, queek.

**Mother Dolphin:** Eeeek ooh, eeerk. Squeak-squeak eeeek, ahoa squeak?

**Baby Dolphin:**   Eerk squeak.

**Mother Dolphin:** Week aeek squeak.  Ahoa ereeek ooheek, squeak eeeek.

**Baby Dolphin:**   Eek, eek?

**Mother Dolphin:** Eweeeek.  Eeeeeh oeeek, squeak.

**Baby Dolphin:**   Eeeeho.

## Translation

**Mother Dolphin:** _____

**Baby Dolphin:** _____

**Mother Dolphin:** _____

**Baby Dolphin:** _____

**Mother Dolphin:** _____

**Baby Dolphin:** _____

**Mother Dolphin:** _____

**Baby Dolphin:** _____

**Name** _____ **Date** _____

# Dolphins of Another Age

**Directions:** Scientists believe that more than 60 million years ago dolphins were mammals that lived on land just like humans. However, they looked different before they adapted to living in the water.  One of the ways they adapted to life in the water is that their front legs became flippers and their back legs disappeared altogether.  Draw a picture of a dolphin as you think it might have looked when it lived on land.  Then, answer questions about the land-living dolphin.

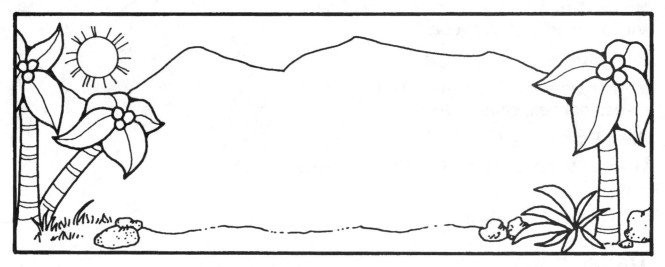

1. When the predecessor to the dolphin lived on land, what do you think it ate?

   _____

2. Do you think it was still a mammal?  If so, what were some of the characteristics that made it a mammal?

   _____

   _____

3. How much do you think dolphins have changed in size from when they lived on land?  Are they smaller now, or were they smaller when they lived on land?

   _____

   _____

**Name** _____ **Date** _____

# How Deep Is the Ocean?

**Directions:** Read the chart below on ocean depth and answer the questions that follow.

| Ocean | Average Depth | Deepest Point (meters) |
|---|---|---|
| Arctic Ocean | 1,200 m | 5,450 m |
| Atlantic Ocean | 3,300 m | 9,560 m |
| Southern Ocean | 3,730 m | 8,260 m |
| Indian Ocean | 3,900 m | 8,800 m |
| Pacific Ocean | 4,150 m | 11,328 m |

1. As one goes deeper, the sea gets darker and colder. At 1,000 meters, there is no sunlight at all. Considering the average depth of the ocean, is more water above 1,000 meters or is more below 1,000 meters?

   _____

2. How many feet are in a meter?

   _____

3. How many feet (meters) deep is the Pacific Ocean?

   _____

4. Which ocean has the deepest point?

   _____

5. Which ocean overall is the deepest?

   _____

6. The average depth of this ocean is less than 2,000 meters. What is it?

   _____

**Name** _____ **Date** _____

# Show Time!

**Directions:** Pretend that you are a famous environmentalist who is an expert on the life of the dolphin. You have been called by a television station for an interview. Answer the following questions.

**Interviewer:** How did you become interested in the dolphin?

**Famous Dolphin Expert:** _____

_____

**Interviewer:** Why do you think the dolphin is such a special mammal?

**Famous Dolphin Expert:** _____

_____

**Interviewer:** What can we do to help protect the dolphins?

**Famous Dolphin Expert:** _____

_____

**Interviewer:** Do you think we need any laws to help protect the dolphin?

**Famous Dolphin Expert:** _____

_____

**Interviewer:** What research questions do you feel are still important for us to address in order to learn more about the dolphin?

**Famous Dolphin Expert:** _____

_____

Now it's your turn to make up both the interview questions and the answers.

**Interviewer:** _____

_____

**Famous Dolphin Expert:** _____

_____

**Interviewer:** _____

_____

**Famous Dolphin Expert:** _____

# *The Manatee*

**Author:** Jean H. Sibbald

**Publisher:** Dillon Press, Inc., 1990.

**Summary:** This book describes the manatee, its habitat, its habits, and the threat that humans pose to its existence. It includes a story about some of the experiences of a manatee named "Success" and her calf.

## Pre-reading Activity

Ask the children if they know what a manatee is. Have they ever seen a manatee? Show them a picture of a manatee from the book. What does it look like to them?

## Key Concepts:

- sirens
- barnacles
- pollution
- habitat

- aquatic
- herbivorous
- refuges
- migration

- species
- extinct
- research
- muzzle

## Post-reading Questions

1. The manatee eats a lot of plant food, rests a lot, and gives milk to its young. What land animal does this seem similar to? *(A cow; in fact, the manatee has been called a "sea cow.")*

2. How big are manatees? How long are they, and how much do they weigh? *(9 to 13 feet long; 800 to 3,500 pounds)*

3. The manatee swims around in the water all the time. Is the manatee a fish? *(Not at all; it is closely related to the elephant.)*

4. What happened to the manatee-like animal called Steller's sea cow? *(It was hunted to extinction by humans.)*

# *The Manatee* (cont.)

## Post-reading Questions (cont.)

5. What is the greatest danger to manatees? *(Boats crash into manatees or cut them with their propellers.)*

6. What can we do to help protect the manatees? *(We can set up refuges for them and educate boaters to stay away from them and to drive their boats slowly, etc.)*

7. Do you think the manatee can be saved from extinction? *(Answers may vary.)*

## Learning Activities

- There are many people who do not know much about the manatee. Create a list of true and false items about the manatee, using page 93.

- Manatees reach 9 to 13 feet in length and can weigh up to 3,000 pounds. Ask students to make a list of mammals that are about the same size as the manatee.

- Ask students to re-read the book and identify the mammal that is the closest relative to the manatee. On page 94, identify ways in which the manatee and the elephant are the same and different.

- In the state of Florida, people can purchase license plates that have a picture of manatee on them. The additional money for the purchase of this license plate is used to save the manatees. Ask students to make a list of activities that people in the state of Florida can use the money for to help save the manatees.

- The name of the manatee's new baby is "Successful." Ask students to write stories about the life of Successful during her first year. Remind them to consider her travels, food, and relationship with her mother and the herd. Ask students to use the following vocabulary words when writing their stories:

  - weaning
  - herbivorous
  - migration
  - feeding habits
  - habitat
  - predator
  - barnacle

- Did you know that motorboaters are a dangerous predator to the manatee? Think of several ways in which motorboaters harm the manatee and what they can do to prevent this. Ask students to design a notice to be distributed to the motorboaters at yacht clubs along the seacoast where manatees live. Remember, this notice should capture the attention of the motorboaters, as well as provide them with facts and information about what to do. Patterns to help students are provided on page 96.

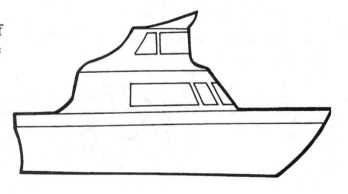

**Name** _____**Date**_____

# The Manatee: True or False Facts

**Directions:** Create a list of true and false facts about the manatee.

1. The manatee is an aggressive animal which
   will attack other animals if it feels it will be harmed.        True        False

2. The manatee is often referred to as the West Indian
   manatee because it lives in waterways from Brazil
   to Virginia in the United States.        True        False

3. _____        True        False

   _____

4. _____        True        False

   _____

5. _____        True        False

   _____

6. _____        True        False

   _____

7. _____        True        False

   _____

8. _____        True        False

   _____

9. _____        True        False

   _____

10. _____        True        False

    _____

11. _____        True        False

    _____

12. _____        True        False

    _____

**Name**_____**Date**_____

# Manatee And Elephant: Compare and Contrast

**Directions:** List several ways in which the manatee and the elephant are alike and different. Be sure to consider their color, size, food, where they live, and behavior. Two examples have been completed.

| Manatee | Elephant | Choices | |
|---|---|---|---|
| 1. mobile and covers a lot of territory | 1. mobile and covers a lot of territory | (Same) | Different |
| 2. is a small to medium-sized mammal | 2. is a large mammal | Same | (Different) |
| 3. | 3. | Same | Different |
| 4. | 4. | Same | Different |
| 5. | 5. | Same | Different |
| 6. | 6. | Same | Different |
| 7. | 7. | Same | Different |
| 8. | 8. | Same | Different |
| 9. | 9. | Same | Different |
| 10. | 10. | Same | Different |

# Suggested Comparisons and Contrasts

## Comparisons

1. Both are mammals.

2. Both breathe air with lungs.

3. Both have some body hair.

4. Both are warm blooded.

5. Both feed their young milk.

6. Both are gentle and typically not aggressive.

7. Both are highly mobile and cover large amounts of territory.

8. Both eat vegetation.

9. Both are the same color with similarly textured skin.

10. Both have bulls who lead large herds.

11. Both face extinction because of man.

## Contrasts

1. Manatees live in the water, but elephants live on land.

2. Manatees have flippers rather than legs like the elephant.

3. Manatees have a snout rather than a trunk.

4. Elephants are larger than manatees.

5. Elephants have tusks but manatees do not.

**Name** _____ **Date** _____

# Attention Motorboaters!

**Directions:** Develop a notice to be distributed to motorboaters at yacht clubs along the coast where manatees live. Be sure to include information about what is harmful to manatees and what they can do to help. Use the patterns provided to help create your notice.

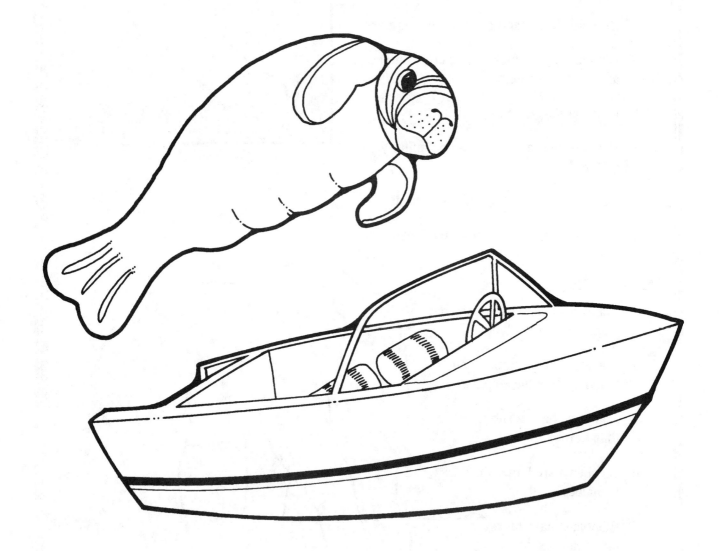

# Watching Whales

**Author:** John F. Waters

**Illustrator:** Illustrated with photographs

**Publisher:** Cobblehill Books/Dutton, 1991.

**Summary:** This book is about a fifth grade class which "adopts" a whale and then takes an excursion from Provinceton, Massachusetts, to go whale watching. Information on how to adopt a whale is provided at the end of the book.

## Pre-reading Activity

Have any of the children gone out in a boat on the ocean? How exciting do they think it would be to see whales swimming by? Show them the cover of the book, which portrays a humpback whale breaching or throwing itself up above the surface of the water. Discuss what it would be like to see this.

## Key Concepts:

- tail flukes
- plankton
- baleen
- blowhole

- breaching
- Provincetown
- migration
- mammal

- flippers
- spouting
- whale songs
- sounding

## Post-reading Questions

1. Why is Provincetown a good place to take a boat to watch whales? *(It is near a place called Stellwagen Bank which has many fish and other nutrients for whales. It is also on the route of their migration.)*

2. How many different kinds of whales can you name? *(blue, finback, gray, humpback, killer, minke, right, orca, sperm)*

3. What does it mean to "adopt" a whale? *(The students select a whale from among those available for adoption. The class must pay a fee which helps support research on whales. The class receives a certificate of adoption, a photograph of its whale, and a migration map. Information is sent to the class about its whale, such as sightings and births.)*

# *Watching Whales* (cont.)

## Post-reading Questions (cont.)

4. There are only a few hundred right whales still in existence out of thousands. What happened to them? *(Whalers have hunted and killed whales for many years, particularly the right whale. Now many countries have outlawed whaling, but a few still hunt whales.)*

5. What are some of the things whales do when they are swimming that people like to see? *(They "sound" or dive; they "spout" or blow mist and air out of their blowholes; they "breach" or lunge out of the water; and they "head slap" or slap their heads down on the water.)*

6. How can individual whales be told from each other? *(Each whale's tail flukes are different, like fingerprints.)*

7. Why do you think seeing a whale would be such a special event? *(Answers may vary.)*

## Learning Activities

• Ask students to work in small groups and to write to the following groups that offer "adopt-a-whale" programs. After the materials arrive, select the organization from which the class would like to adopt a whale. Students can earn money for adoption through class projects. If possible, adopt more than one whale.

### Adopt-a-Whale Organizations:

**Whale Adoption Project**
PO Box 388
North Falmouth, MA 02556

**Pacific Whale Foundation**
Kealia Beach Plaza, Suite 21
101 North Kihei Road
Kihei, Maui, HI 96753

**Adopt a Whale Fund**
BIOS (Brior Island Ocean Study)
Westport, Digby County
Nova Scotia, Canada B0V 1H0

**Orca Adoption Program**
PO Box 945
Friday Harbor, WA 98250

**The Finback Catalogue**
College of the Atlantic
Bar Harbor, ME 04609

**Right Whale Program**
New England Aquarium
Central Wharf
Boston, MA 02110

# *Watching Whales* (cont.)

## Learning Activities (cont.)

- Ask students to select a type of whale about which they would like to have more information. Ask them to write a 200-word description of the whale they select. Students who select similar whales can then form a group and compile their papers in one report to be read to the class. Types of whales include: gray whale, killer whale, right whale, orca whale, finback whale, and humpback whale.

- There are five major oceans of the world. Ask students to complete page 100 about our oceans.

- The whale is not the only endangered sea animal; there are many others. Ask students to complete page 101 to learn about other sea animals that are endangered.

- Narwhals live in the Arctic Ocean and are members of the whale family. They are different from other whales in one way: they have only two teeth growing out of their upper lip. Male narwhals have one tooth that grows in a spiral that can be as long as 9 feet. Have students draw a picture of a male narwhal with its spiraled, long tooth jutting out of its upper lip.

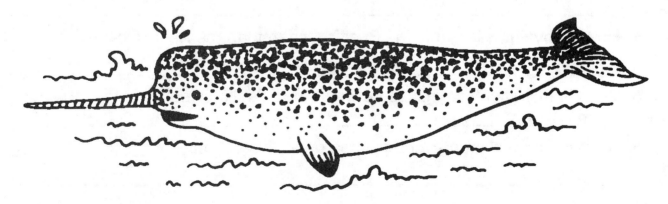

- Ask students to complete page 102 to learn about blue whales.

**Name** _____**Date**_____

# The World's Oceans

**Directions:** Use the provided information to answer the questions that follow.

| Ocean | Area in Square Miles |
|---|---|
| Atlantic Ocean | 82,217,000 |
| Pacific Ocean | 166,241,000 |
| Southern Ocean | 35,000,000 |
| Arctic Ocean | 12,257,000 |
| Indian Ocean | 73,600,000 |

1. List the oceans in order from the largest to the smallest. _____

   _____

   _____

   _____

2. Name the three smallest oceans. _____

   _____

   _____

3. Add up the area of the three smallest oceans. _____

   Is this total area smaller or greater than that of the largest ocean?

   _____

4. How many times larger is the Pacific Ocean than the Arctic Ocean?

   _____

5. What is the difference in size between the Atlantic Ocean and the Indian
   Ocean? _____

6. What is the total area encompassed by all five oceans? _____

   _____

   _____

**Name** _____**Date**_____

# Endangered Sea Animals

**Directions:** Use books from the library, encyclopedias, etc., to discover several more facts about each of these endangered sea animals.

| Sea Animal | Information | Facts |
|---|---|---|
| **blue whale** | The blue whale lives largely in the Southern Ocean, and originally there were more than 250,000 of them. Today there are as few as 11,000. | |
| **finback whale** | Originally, there were more than 500,000, and now there are fewer than 120,000. | |
| **Kent Ridley turtle** | We are unsure how many of these turtles are left. They live in the Gulf of Mexico, but they are killed for their meat, shells, and eggs. | |
| **Florida manatee** | Fewer than 1,000 are left. | |
| **Juan Fernandez fur seal** | It is one of the rarest seals with only 705 left. | |
| **sea otter** | Hunted for its fur, the sea otter's numbers are rising because it has been protected in the last few years. | |
| **monk seal** | It is Europe's most endangered mammal. There are fewer than 500 left. | |

**Name** _____**Date**_____

# A Whale of a Whale

**Directions:** Use the information about blue whales to answer the questions that follow.

- The blue whale is the largest sea animal.
- The blue whale is the biggest animal that has ever existed.
- The blue whale is the largest animal on earth.
- A blue whale can weigh up to 150 tons (more than 40 rhinoceroses).
- The tongue of a blue whale weighs 3 tons (more than 35 men).
- The baby blue whale is the biggest baby of any animal.
- A baby blue whale weighs five tons (more than an adult elephant).
- A baby blue whale weighs more than 1,000 human babies.
- A baby blue whale drinks 132 gallons of mother's milk a day.
- When a baby blue whale is six months old, it weighs about 20 tons.

1. A killer whale is larger than a blue whale.          True     False
2. A baby whale is not a mammal.          True     False
3. A baby blue whale drinks milk from its mother.          True     False
4. When a baby blue whale is six months old, what fraction of its full growth is it?

   _____

5. How many gallons of mother's milk does a baby blue whale drink in a week?

   _____

6. On the back of this sheet, draw a picture of a baby blue whale. On top of the baby blue whale, draw a picture of a human being about the size it would be relative to the baby blue whale.

   _____

7. Make up your own question about blue whales and write the answer.

   _____

# *On the Brink of Extinction: The California Condor*

**Author:** Caroline Arnold

**Photographer:** Michael Wallace

**Publisher:** Harcourt, Brace, Jovanovich, Publishers, 1993.

**Summary:** This book describes the history of the North American condor and details the efforts to capture and breed the few remaining California condors to save them from extinction. The book contains magnificently vivid photographs.

## Pre-reading Activity

Show the students the cover of the book and read its title. Then, record what students say they know about the California condors. As an assignment, ask them to work in groups to research the condor. Allow several days for them to complete this assignment and then to share their findings with what they originally knew about condors. Finally, share with them the book, *On the Brink of Extinction: The California Condor.*

## Key Concepts:

- extinction
- captive breeding
- talons
- vulture
- predators
- incubators
- condominiums
- fledged
- AC-9
- carcass
- candling
- pip

## Post-reading Questions

1. Why didn't condors disappear in California as they did everywhere else in North America? *(Answers may include the fact that they had fish and other sea animals that washed up on the beach to eat.)*

2. Describe what a full-grown California condor looks like. *(Answers might include that it has a wingspan of about 10 feet, weighs as much as 23 ½ pounds, has new feathers on its head or neck, has a creamy yellow or orange skin on its head, and has black feathers on its body except for a row of white under the wings.)*

# *On the Brink of Extinction: The California Condor* (cont.)

## Post-reading Questions (cont.)

3. What caused the condors to become "on the brink of extinction"? *(Answers might include that they were shot for sport and for museum exhibits; they died from eating poisons put out for coyotes; their habitats were reduced; they collided with power lines, etc.)*

4. What is being done to ensure the continuation of the California condor? *(Answers might include that the Los Angeles Zoo and San Diego Wild Animal Park have built sheltered breeding areas that are monitored carefully; scientists continue to study and develop plans for returning captive condors to the wild, etc.)*

5. Why is it so important to preserve the condor? *(Answers may vary.)*

6. How are baby condors fed in captivity? *(At first they are fed by humans and then by condor-shaped puppets.)* Why are they fed by puppets? *(to fool the young condor into believing it is being fed by its parent so that it can adjust more easily to life in the wild when it is released)*

## Learning Activities

- Incubators and fertilized eggs are available in many pet stores. If possible, purchase the necessary supplies to enable students to observe how eggs hatch. Allow students time to observe the eggs each day and to record their observations (page 105).

- As a group, write a letter to Caroline Arnold and/or Michael Wallace telling them what you liked about their book, what you learned, and why a book such as this is important. Contact them through their publisher.

- Duplicate and distribute copies of the crossword puzzle (page 106) to the students and ask them to complete it. Allow time to check answers or supply an answer key.

- Ask students to follow the instructions on page 107 to write a cinquain poem about the condor. Allow time to share the poems.

- Ask the students to create posters depicting the plight of the condor (page 108). Once they are completed, display the posters around the school in order to create an awareness about the condors.

- Many people are involved in helping to preserve and protect the condor. Discuss and list all the different related jobs. Ask students to write a brief paragraph telling whether or not they would like to have any of the positions discussed and why. Allow time to share.

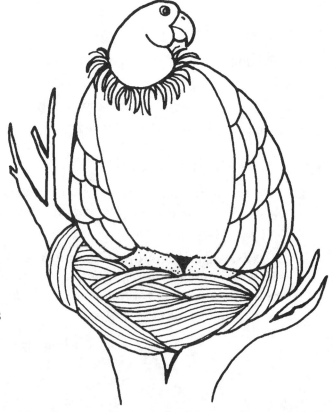

# Egg Hatching Observation Record

Number of Eggs _____

Type of Eggs _____

**Directions:** When it is your turn to be recorder, observe the eggs and write down any changes that you see.

| Date | Activity/Observation Notes | Name of Recorder |
|------|----------------------------|------------------|
|      |                            |                  |
|      |                            |                  |
|      |                            |                  |
|      |                            |                  |
|      |                            |                  |
|      |                            |                  |

**Name** _____ **Date** _____

# Condor Crossword

Complete the crossword puzzle, using the words in the box to help you with the clues.

| carcass | egg tooth | incubators |
| condorminiums | condor tags | fledged |
| talons | candling | pip |
| extinction | captive breeding | predator |

**Across**

2. A body of a dead animal
3. The name for the condor pens at the zoo
5. When the bird leaves the nest for first time
7. Claws on the condors
8. First crack in egg
10. Something that preys on others
11. Machines that keep eggs warm so they can hatch

12. Hard knot on top of beak that makes first crack in egg

**Down**

1. Eventual disappearance of a species
4. Holding eggs to a bright light to see inside egg
6. Mating condors while in captivity
9. A way of identifying condors

*Endangered Species*

**Name** _____ **Date** _____

# Condor Cinquain

**Directions:** Write a cinquain about the condor, following the guidelines below. Place your poem inside the condor.

**Line 1:** one word (the title)

**Line 2:** two words (describing the title)

**Line 3:** three words (an action)

**Line 4:** four words (a feeling)

**Line 5:** one word (relating to the title)

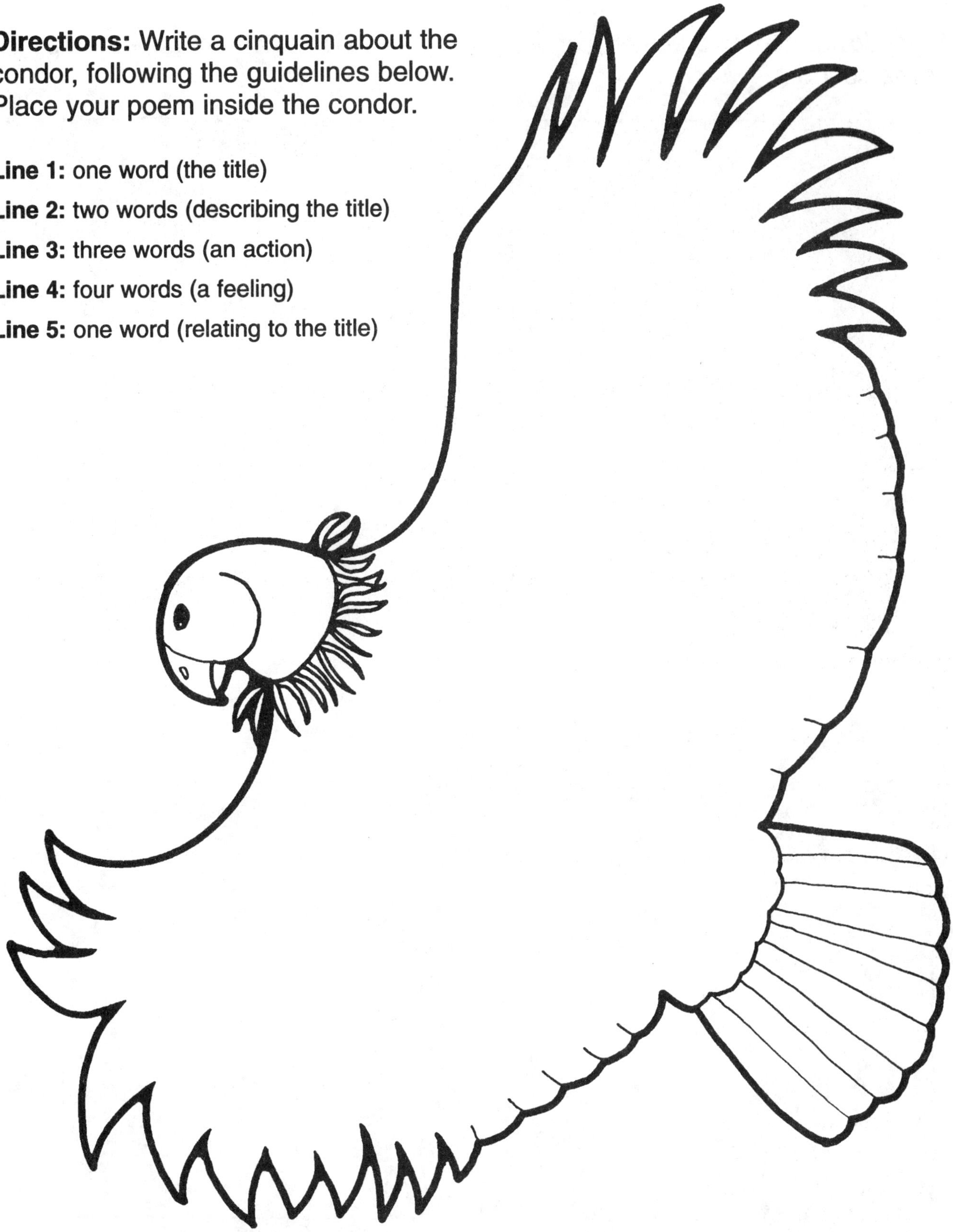

**Name** _____**Date** _____

# Plight of the Condor

**Directions:** Create a poster that will send a message to others about the plight of the condor.

# Gray Wolf, Red Wolf

**Author:** Dorothy Hinshaw Patent

**Photographer:** William Munoz

**Publisher:** Clarion Books, 1990.

**Summary:** This book provides beautiful, vivid photographs along with descriptions of the characteristics, life cycles, and behaviors of the gray and red wolves. In addition, the author provides species information about the re-introduction of wolves to Yellowstone National Park.

## Pre-reading Activity

Show the students the inside cover picture of the wolf and read the paragraph on the back cover of the book. Then, ask the students to organize into two debate teams and react to the statement that "Hunted to the edge of extinction, [wolves] have begun to make a comeback, but their presence has sparked a heated controversy between environmentalists who are pleased to see the wolves return and others who would prefer that these animals stay away forever."

## Key Concepts:

- omega male and female
- parvo virus
- ecosystems
- beta animal
- Canis lupus
- predators
- captivity
- bounty
- subspecies
- preying
- captive breeding
- alpha male and female
- scent gland
- Canis rufus
- domesticated
- pecking order

## Post-reading Questions

1. What are the differences between a wolf and a dog? *(Answers may vary but might include wolves' legs are longer, chests narrower, and their feet bigger. Wolf tails hang down, and dog tails often curl up. Wolves have scent glands, and dogs do not.)*

2. What are wolf territories? *(an area within which the wolf lives, dens, and hunts)* How large is a wolf's territory? *(anywhere from 25 sq. miles to 540 sq. miles in size)* How do they know their territories? *(Boundaries are carefully marked by urine.)*

# *Gray Wolf, Red Wolf* (cont.)

## Post-reading Questions *(cont.)*

3. What are some ways in which wolves communicate? *(Answers might include body postures, scent marking, howling, growling, and whining in individual "voices.")*

4. How did scientists monitor the red wolves that were set free in the wild? *(Adults wore special collars fitted with radio transmitters, and the pups had radio transmitters put inside their abdomens).*

5. Explain the goal of the Red Wolf Recovery Plan. *(The goal is to have 223 red wolves in the wild and 330 in captivity.)* Do you support this plan? Why or why not? *(Answers may vary.)*

6. Why are wolves hunted? *(Their fur is used for coats and rugs, and it keeps the game populations high for human hunters.)*

## Learning Activities

- Invite the students to think about the fact that wolves certainly do behave as animals; however, they also have some almost human qualities. Ask them to complete page 112 and then compare and contrast their answers.

- Obtain a copy and view the video *Winter Wolf* (1992, 30 minutes, available for $19.95 from Wehman Video, 2366 Eastlake Ave. E., Ste 420, Seattle, WA 98102). It is about a Native American girl who assists a scientist and also learns from her grandmother's earlier experience with a wolf.

- Ask the students to create an environmental impact statement and poster that could be presented to Congress (page 113). Collect these statements and mail them along with a cover letter to Defenders of Wildlife, 1244 Nineteenth St. NW, Washington, DC 20036.

- Divide the students into committees and divide the organizations listed on page 64 in *Gray Wolf, Red Wolf* among the committees. Committees are to contact the organizations and then make a display of the materials they receive.

# Gray Wolf, Red Wolf *(cont.)*

## Learning Activities *(cont.)*

- Sayings about wolves have been passed down over the years such as "He is a wolf in sheep's clothing" and "He cried wolf once too often." Ask the students to explain the meanings of these sayings. Do they know any others?

  Collect additional nonfiction books about wolves, such as:

  > ***To the Top of the World: Adventures with Arctic Wolves*** by Jim Brandenburg (Walker, 1993)

  > ***The Moon of the Gray Wolves*** by Jean Craighead George (Harper Collins, 1991)

  > ***Wolves*** by Seymour Simon (Harper Collins, 1993)

  > ***Wolf Magic for Kids*** by Tom Wolpert (Gareth Stevens, 1991)

- Provide time for the students to read these books and then ask them to complete page 114. Then, divide students into small groups for sharing. In addition, use a map of the Northern Hemisphere and ask the students to identify the range of the wolf today, as well as in the past.

- As a culminating activity, invite a group of younger children to a "Learn About Wolves Day." Students could work in various committees as they prepare for the day. Activities might include dressing like a wolf, reading folk tales such as *Little Red Riding Hood* or *The Three Little Pigs*, playing the music of *Peter and the Wolf,* and, finally, presenting factual information about the wolf through posters, skits, puppet shows, etc.

Scene from *Peter and the Wolf*

Name _____ Date _____

# Wolves v. Humans

Although wolves have mainly animal-like qualities, they also have some human-like qualities. Think about qualities attributed to wolves and list them under the appropriate column.

| Animal-like Qualities | Human-like Qualities |
| --- | --- |
| _____ | _____ |
| _____ | _____ |
| _____ | _____ |
| _____ | _____ |
| _____ | _____ |
| _____ | _____ |

What are some additional myths you have learned about through reading a variety of folklore about wolves? In what ways are the wolves you have read about in folk tales human-like or animal-like? Explain your answer.

_____

_____

_____

_____

_____

_____

_____

**Name** _____ **Date** _____

# Environmental Impact Statement

**Directions:** The book *Gray Wolf, Red Wolf* mentions that before any wolves can be transplanted to Yellowstone National Park, an environmental impact statement must be prepared. This statement needs to address all aspects of wolf re-introduction, including the growth of wolf population, the risk to farmers' livestock, and the effects on park deer, elk, and bison. Create an environmental impact statement and then design a poster in the box below that will support the statement.

| Environmental Impact Statement | Support Poster |
|---|---|
|  |  |

**Name** _____**Date**_____

# All About Wolves

**Directions:** After you have read *Gray Wolf, Red Wolf* and other nonfiction books about wolves, provide the following information.

**What I know about wolves:**

_____

_____

_____

_____

_____

_____

_____

**What I would like to know about wolves:**

_____

_____

_____

_____

_____

_____

_____

_____

_____

# *Project Panda*

**Author:** Jill Bailey

**Illustrator:** Alan Baker

**Publisher:** Steck-Vaughn Co., 1992.

**Summary:** The endangered giant panda and its diet, breeding habits, and habitat are fully described through text and illustrations. In addition, the efforts of Chinese environmentalists working to save the panda from extinction are presented.

## Pre-reading Activity

Read the brief biographical sketches of the three main characters found on the back cover of the book. Ask the students to project how these three characters might interact with each other in the text.

## Key Concepts:

- panda
- bamboo
- foresters
- musk deer
- panda reserves
- dung
- haunches
- snub-nosed monkey
- Panda Research Center
- panda rescue squad
- snare
- scent post
- tracking
- radio collars

## Post-reading Questions

1. What can scientists learn from looking at the panda's dung? *(They know what kind of bamboo the panda is eating, the panda's age, whether the panda has worms or parasites, and if it has been eating bamboo rats.)*

2. What do pandas need in order to survive? *(They need lots of bamboo and water.)*

3. Who are the panda's closet relatives? *(Answers might include that no one is sure; however, many believe them to be bears. The panda also may be closely related to the red panda or the raccoon.)*

# *Project Panda* (cont.)

## Post-reading Questions (cont.)

4.  Why is it difficult to save pandas from extinction? *(Answers might include that they need large amounts of bamboo to survive; they eat only one or two species of bamboo; they breed very slowly because they are able to mate only three days every year; and they are hunted for their skins.)*

5.  How do pandas mark their areas or territory? *(They do this by scratching the bark off a tree trunk and then rubbing the liquid produced under their tails onto the tree trunk.)*

6.  What are the Chinese people doing to preserve pandas? *(Answers might include banning all hunting of pandas creating special panda reserves, and cooperating with the World Wildlife Federation's "Save the Panda" campaign.)*

## Learning Activities

*   Provide students with an outline map of China (page 117) and a detailed map of China. Help students locate and label the following: Sichuan province, Gansu province, Shaanxi province, Beijing, Hong Kong.

*   There are many varieties of bamboo growing in China, but pandas feed on only one or two varieties. Ask the students to research other uses of bamboos and then to share their findings.

*   There are many animals that are endangered. Steck-Vaughn has a series of books available that addresses this problem; find them in the library and make them available to students.

*   Ask the students to reflect on the book *Project Panda* and to create a related diamante poem (page 118). Allow students to share poems.

*   Reinforce the key concepts of *Project Panda* by asking students to complete page 119.

*   Protecting the panda from extinction appears to be a difficult and expensive task. Divide the students into two groups for a debate with one team advocating more resources for saving the panda and the other for limiting resources for saving the panda. Remind the students that although they may not actually support the side they are assigned, the important thing is to provide all the facts.

**Name** _____**Date**_____

# Mapping China

**Directions:** Locate and label the following places on the map below.

- Sichuan province
- Beijing
- Gansu province

- Hong Kong
- Shaanxi province
- Nanking

*Add additional cities, rivers, provinces, etc., with which you are familiar.

**Map of China**

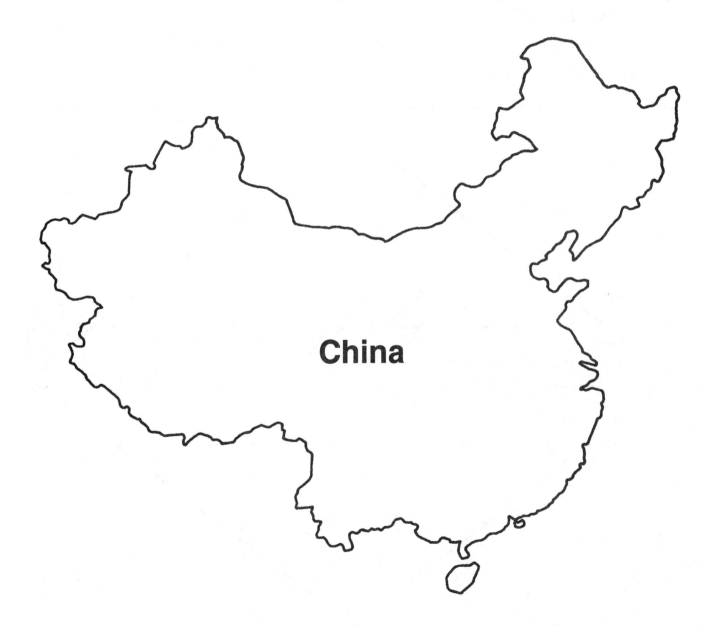

China

**Name** _____**Date**_____

# Panda Diamante

**Directions:** A diamante poem is so-called because of its diamond shape. Follow the guideline below for writing a diamante poem about the giant panda and then illustrate it on separate paper.

**Line 1:** one word (a noun or a pronoun)

**Line 2:** two words (adjectives describing line 1)

**Line 3:** three words ("ing" verbs showing action related to line 1)

**Line 4:** four words (nouns, the first two relating to line 1 and the last two to line 7)

**Line 5:** three words ("ing" verbs showing action related to line 7)

**Line 6:** two words (adjectives describing line 7)

**Line 7:** one word (a noun or pronoun, often the opposite of the word in line 1)

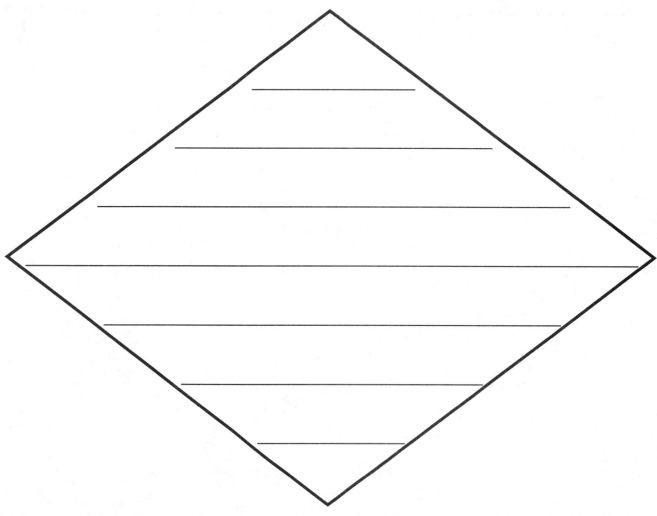

**Name** _____ **Date** _____

# Panda Fact

**Directions:** Match the words and phrases in the box below with the words that follow. Then, write a sentence using each new word.

A. a way of finding pandas

B. sends out signals that can be picked up on a radio

C. an animal that shares the forest with the panda

D. a trap

E. a place where pandas are studied

F. someone who hunts illegally

G. a way in which pandas communicate with each other

H. an animal that hunters are trapping

I. food panda eats

1. ____bamboo  _____

2. ____poachers  _____

3. ____radio collars  _____

4. ____scent post  _____

5. ____snare  _____

6. ____panda research center _____

7. ____snub-nosed monkey  _____

8. ____musk deer  _____

9. ____tracking  _____

# Forests

# Tropical Rain Forests Around the World

**Author:** Elaine Landau

**Publisher:** Franklin Watts, 1990.

**Summary:** This book explains the environmental conditions of rain forests in different parts of the world. It describes the plants, animals, and humans who live in them and the threat of deforestation.

## Pre-reading Activity

Read the title of the book and write "rain forests" on the chalkboard. Ask the students to discuss what they know about rain forests as you create a web.

## Post-reading Activities

1. What kinds of animals live in the rain forest? *(Monkeys and apes, anteaters, and tapirs are representative. Some of these, including the orangutan, are endangered species.)*

2. Why are tropical rain forests important? *(Many of our foods such as bananas, corn, and chocolate first came from rain forests, as do many medicines. Some doctors think many new medicines can be found in rain forest plants. The rain forests produce oxygen for us to breathe. The burning of the rain forests pollutes the air and can lead to global warming.)*

3. Why do you think people are uprooting and burning the tropical rain forests? *(People come into the rain forest and cut down trees for lumber or to clear the land for crops or for raising livestock.)*

4. What do you think happens to the land after deforestation? *(The animals die or run away, and the other plants die out or are burned up. The soil of the former rain forest is not suited for agriculture and soon erodes away, leaving an area not suited for anything. The people then move to another area of the rain forest and often ruin it, as well.)*

# Tropical Rain Forests Around the World *(cont.)*

## Learning Activities

- Divide the students into five groups and assign the names of 3–5 environmental agencies and organizations that they should contact for literature and information. When they receive information, they can compile it into a booklet that can be shared with the other groups. A list of the environmental agencies and organizations concerned with rain forests follows.

**American Forest Institute**
1619 Massachusetts Avenue NW
Washington, DC 20036

**Center for Population Options**
1012 14th Street NW
Suite 1200
Washington, DC 20005

**Environmental Action**
1346 Connecticut Avenue, NW
Washington, DC 20036

**Environmental Action Coalition**
235 East 49th Street
New York, NY 10017

**Environmental Defense Fund**
257 Park Avenue-South
New York, NY 10010

**Environmental Law Institute**
Suite 200
1616 P Street NW
Washington, DC 20036

**Environmental Project on Central America**
349 Church Street
San Francisco, CA 94114

**Friends of the Earth**
124 Spear Street
San Francisco, CA 94105

**Global Greenhouse Network**
1130 17th Street NW
Washington, DC, 20036

**Greenpeace**
2007 R Street, NW
Washington, DC 20009

**Rain Forest Alliance**
295 Madison Avenue
New York, NY 10017

**Rain Forest Action Network**
301 Broadway
San Francisco, CA 94133

**NRDC Atmospheric Protection Initiative**
Suite 300
A1350 New York Avenue, NW
Washington, DC 20005

**Nature Conservancy**
1800 N. Kent Street
Arlington, VA 22209

- Today the rain forest is being destroyed at a rapid rate that is devastating. This devastation will affect not just the area near the rain forest but the entire world and planet. Many of these problems have potential solutions. Ask students to use library reference books to complete page 124, which is designed to identify problems with the rain forest, the effects, and the solutions. Several problems have been identified for them. They will also need to identify two additional problems.

- One hundred million years ago, rain forests grew in many places where they are not today. Ask students to identify several places in the world in which rain forests once existed and now do not. (*Answers: Norway, Sweden, Russia*) Now identify several places in the world where rain forests presently exist. (*Answers: New Guinea, Malaysia, Africa, Burma, Indonesia, South America*)

# *Tropical Rain Forests Around the World* (cont.)

## Learning Activities (cont.)

- Ask students whether they know that each year every person in the United States consumes enough items made from wood to equal a tree 100 feet tall and 16 inches in diameter. Since there are approximately 230 million people who live in the United States, that add up to over 230 million trees a year. Page 125 asks students to identify several items made from wood and to suggest alternatives that would eliminate the need for cutting down so many trees.

- Ask students to design two postcards, one showing the rain forest before slash-and-burn and one showing the rain forest after slash-and-burn (page 126). They can write messages on the postcards and mail them to their Congressional representatives.

- There are so many plants and insects in the rain forest that some have yet to be discovered. On page 127, create a picture of a plant and an insect that you imagine lives in the rain forest. Since you are creating these two, you can also create names for them and information about them.

- Over 200 million adults and children live in tropical rain forests. The way most of them live is very different from the way you live. Write a story of a boy or girl your age who lives in the rain forest. In the story, include the following information: (a) the boy's or girl's name, (b) the names of his/her parents, brothers, and sisters, (c) where the boy/girl lives and what his/her shelter looks like, (d) what he/she eats and how it is gathered/grown, and (e) whether he/she goes to school or how he/she learns about the ways of his/her culture and people.

- Scientists think that burning tropical forests will lead to a change in climate. Some scientists think the Earth will grow warmer by as much as 7 degrees at the poles. Other scientists think that burning tropical forests could block out some of the sun's rays, causing the Earth to become colder. On page 128, ask students to list the consequences for each of these two events.

Name _____ Date_____

# Rain Forest: Problems, Effects, and Solutions

**Directions:** Add information to the boxes below to demonstrate that you understand the problems, effects, and solutions within a rain forest. Five problems have already been identified; you will need to identify two more. You may use reference books to complete the chart.

| Problem | Effect | Solution |
|---|---|---|
| Trees and shrubs are cut down for grazing. | | |
| Trees and shrubs are burned, using slash-and-burn procedures. | | |
| When rain forest land is used for agriculture, animal and bird habitats are destroyed. | | |
| Logging is a serious threat to the rain forests. | | |
| There is a loss of medicines from rain forest plants. | | |
| | | |
| | | |

**Name** _____ **Date** _____

# Amazing but True!

**Think:** Each person consumes enough items made from wood to equal a 100-foot tree.

**Directions:** Listed below are items we use that are made from wood. Next to each item, identify alternative materials or other ways we can reduce our dependence on wood for this item.

Furniture _____

_____

Matches _____

_____

Paper _____

_____

Plastics _____

_____

Rayon _____

_____

Turpentine _____

_____

Cellophane _____

_____

Paper Bags _____

_____

Paper and Plastic Packaging of Food Items _____

_____

Photocopying _____

_____

**Name** _____**Date**_____

# Rain Forest Postcards

**Directions:** Ask each student to design two postcards, one showing the rain forest before slash-and-burn and one showing the rain forest after slash-and-burn. Cut out the postcards and write a message to your representative, explaining why saving the rain forests is important.

**Name** _____ **Date** _____

# Create a Rain Forest Insect and Plant

**Directions:** Draw a picture of an insect and a plant that you imagine live in the rain forest and then provide the requested information.

**My Plant**

**Name:** _____

**Location:** _____

**Size:** _____

How it contributes to the rain forest: _____

Its possible uses by people: _____

What other plants it is related to: _____

Its possible uses by man: _____

**My Insect**

**Name:** _____

**Location:** _____

**Size:** _____

How it contributes to the rain forest: _____

Its possible uses by people: _____

What other insects it is related to: _____

What it eats: _____

What eats it: _____

**Name** _____ **Date** _____

# Warmer Earth, Colder Earth

**Directions:** Some scientists think that by burning tropical rain forests the Earth's climate will change.  Some think that the Earth's weather will change by seven degrees warmer at the poles.  Other scientists feel that burning tropical rain forests will shield the sun's rays and make the Earth colder.  Identify what some of the outcomes would be for either of these events.

## The Earth Gets Warmer

**Consequences:**

1. _____
   _____
2. _____
   _____
3. _____
   _____
4. _____
   _____
5. _____
   _____

## The Earth Gets Colder

**Consequences:**

1. _____
   _____
2. _____
   _____
3. _____
   _____
4. _____
   _____
5. _____
   _____

**Name** _____**Date**_____

# Rain Forest Layers

**Directions:** Illustrate trees, plants, and animals that would be found in each of the following layers of a rain forest.

canopy
_____

understory
_____

forest floor
_____

# *Forests*

**Author:** David Lambert

**Publisher:** Troll Associates, 1990.

**Summary:** *Forests* describes the plant and animal life in different types of forests. It also provides information about people who live in forests, cropping forests, vanishing forests, and saving forests. A fact file about forests is included at the end of the book.

## Pre-reading Activity

Ask the students to describe forests they have visited. What kinds of trees and animals did they see? What did they like most about the forest? Least about the forest?

## Key Concepts:

- taiga
- airplanes
- epiphytes
- prop roots
- conifers
- deciduous
- parasite
- anaconda
- lianas
- canopy
- mangrove
- food chain

## Post-reading Questions

1. Describe what mangroves are like and where mangroves are located. (*Mangrove trees grow along warm, muddy seashores beside the Atlantic, Pacific, and Indian Oceans.*)

2. Describe temperate forests and tell where temperate forests are located. (*Temperate forests grow in mild climates. Trees in temperate forests shed their leaves once a year. They are located in parts of North America, Europe, and China.*)

# *Forests* (cont.)

## Post-reading Questions (cont.)

3. Describe rain forests and tell where they are located. *(A rain forest has many layers of plant and animal life. Rain forests are found on moist lowlands near the equator.)*

4. What survival skills are required by people who live in the rain forests? *(Answers may vary.)*

5. How can we use products from forests without destroying our environment? *(We can replace trees as those we need are cut down.)*

6. Approximately how long does it take for a tree to grow to an appropriate size for cutting? *(at least 40 years)*

7. How did the people of India help to save many of their trees? *(They hugged them until the tree cutters went away.)*

## Learning Activities:

• Ask students to identify one type of forest presented in this book and to complete the report on page 133. Allow time to share the reports.

• Ask the children to make a pictorial representation of a food chain (page 134). They can use information provided in this book or do additional research on this topic. Allow time to share and explain the food chains they created.

• Ask students to use the descriptions in this book and to do additional research about different types of trees that grow in forests, e.g., conifers, evergreens, etc. Next, go on a field trip to a park or forest and help the children identify the different types of trees. Encourage them to bring to class leaves and samples of needles, pine cones, etc., from the trees in their neighborhood for identification.

• Create a trivia game using the "Fact File" on pages 30 and 31 of *Forest* by David Lambert and any other information the children may have on forests. Help the children create trivia cards by writing statements or questions such as:

```
┌─────────────────────────────────────────────────┐
│                                                 │
│                   Card 1                        │
│                                                 │
│                                                 │
│                                                 │
│   The tallest tree in the U.S. is _____ feet tall.  │
│                                                 │
│                                                 │
└─────────────────────────────────────────────────┘
```

After cards are made, laminate them and put them at a learning center. Be sure to provide an answer sheet to correspond with the card numbers.

# *Forests* *(cont.)*

## Learning Activities *(cont.)*

- Discuss the importance of saving the trees of the world and what can be done to help preserve them. Ask the students to complete page 135.

- It is important that all people, young and old, realize the significance of saving the forests. Make available books about trees that younger children will enjoy and understand such as:

  *At Home in the Rain Forest* by Diane Willow

  *The Great Kapok Tree* by Lynn Cherry

  *Rain Forest* by Helen Cowcher

  *Rain Forest Secrets* by Arthur Dorros

  *Song for the Ancient Forest* by Nancy Luenn

  *Whisper from the Woods* by Victoria Wirth

- The author of *Forests* described how the people in an Indian village saved their trees by hugging them until the woodcutters went away. This movement spread through India. Share the book *The People Who Hugged Trees* by Birgitta Saflund, which is a folk tale about tree hugging in India.

- The author states that many of the creatures of the rain forest never leave the canopy layer. Therefore, until people began exploring the treetops in 1970, many of these creatures had never been seen. Ask the students to use their imaginations to create an imaginary creature that hasn't yet been discovered. Provide a name and description of the imaginary creature on page 136.

**Name** _____ **Date**_____

# Report on a Forest

**Directions:** Complete the following information and then share your report with the class.

1. What type of forest is your report about? _____

2. Geographically, where would this type of forest be found? _____

_____

3. What kind of climate is needed for this forest to survive? _____

_____

4. What kinds of animals/creatures would you find in this forest?_____

_____

5. What products would this forest provide? _____

_____

6. Describe what it would be like to live in this forest. _____

_____

_____

_____

_____

7. Illustrate this forest.

**Name** _____ **Date**_____

# Forest Food Chain

**Directions:** Use the information provided in *Forests* by David Lambert and other resources to create a pictorial representation of the food chain that occurs in forests.

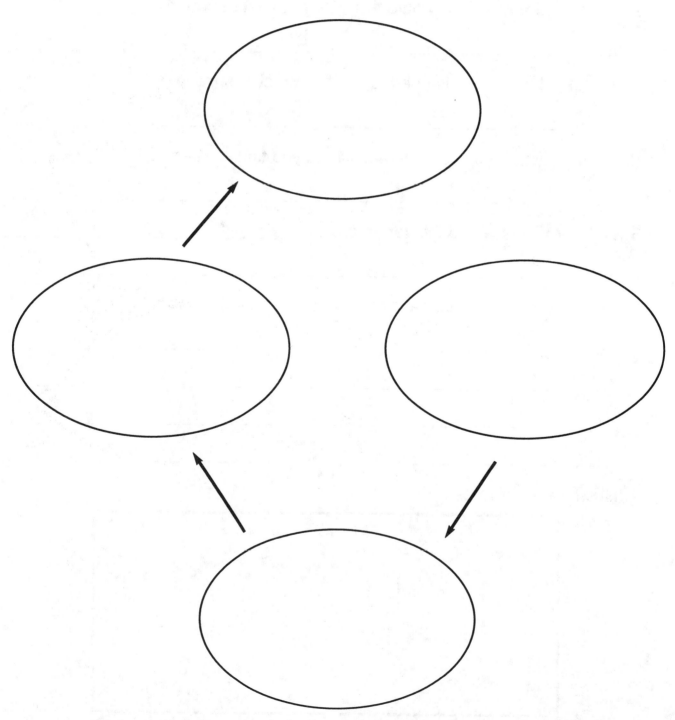

**Name** _____ **Date**_____

# Trees Are Important Because . . .

**Directions:** On each leaf, write a word or phrase explaining why trees are important to our environment.

**Name** _____**Date** _____

# An Imaginary Creature

**Directions:** Create an illustration of an imaginary creature that has not yet been discovered in the rain forest.

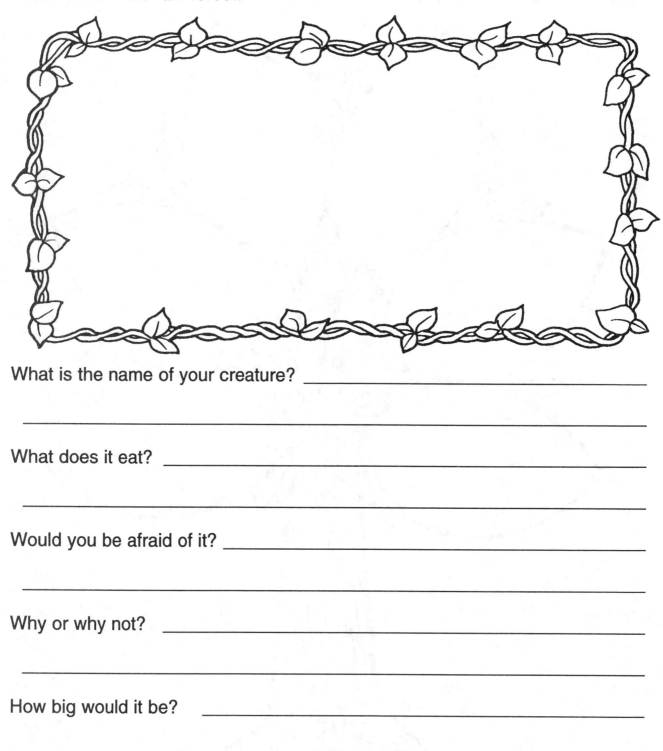

What is the name of your creature? _____

_____

What does it eat? _____

_____

Would you be afraid of it? _____

_____

Why or why not? _____

_____

How big would it be? _____

_____

# Trees and Leaves

**Author:** Althea Braithwaite

**Illustrator:** David More

**Publisher:** Troll Associates, 1990.

**Summary:** This book introduces the reader to the marvelous world of trees, what they are and how they grow, what they produce, and what creatures live in them.

## Pre-reading Activity

Ask the students if they take trees for granted. What kinds of trees live in your area? Can the students recognize them?

## Key Concepts:

- broadleaved
- evergreen
- cambium

- conifer
- photosynthesis
- chlorophyll

- deciduous
- sapwood
- palms

## Post-reading Questions

1. What are the three main types of tree? *(One is the broadleaved tree, most of which are deciduous; that is, they drop their leaves; and then there are conifers, most of which are evergreens; that is, they always have some green leaves; and there are palms, which have a stout stem which unfolds at the top into a crown of fan- or feather-shaped leaves.)*

2. What makes the food for the tree? *(Chlorophyll in the leaves is a green substance that enables the tree to convert carbon dioxide into energy for the food through a process called photosynthesis. At the end of the process, the tree releases oxygen into the air for us and other creatures to breathe.)*

3. Why do leaves turn gold and orange in the autumn? *(To prepare for winter, trees close down their sap supply to the leaves. The green chlorophyll fades, and the fall colors are no longer masked and become visible.)*

4. What are the parts of a tree trunk? *(A trunk has a center of heartwood which is strong and helps keep the tree straight. Each year, a tree grows a new layer of sapwood around the trunk to help carry the sap up the tree. You can tell how old a tree is by counting the number of rings it has.)*

# *Trees and Leaves* (cont.)

## Post-reading Questions (cont.)

5. What kinds of birds and animals live in trees? *(Woodpeckers and owls are two of the main kinds of birds that live in trees, but there are hundreds. In temperate climates, there are many squirrels, and in tropical forests there are monkeys, sloths, and other animals that live in trees.)*

6. Tell about the foods that we get from trees. *(We get nuts such as walnuts, hazelnuts, hickory nuts, Brazil nuts, and cashews and fruits such as apples, pears, plums, and oranges, in addition to coconuts, dates, and olives.)*

7. What do you think the world would be like if there were no trees? *(Answers may vary.)*

## Learning Activities

- Ask students to identify fruit trees that live in or near the area or fruit trees they have in their yards or neighborhood. Tell them to collect a piece of fruit from a local fruit tree or to purchase fruit in a local grocery store. Ask them to bring the fruit to class to plant a tree as directed on page 140.

- Ask students to take a walk in their yards or neighborhood. Tell them to notice the many different kinds of leaves on the trees and on the ground. Ask them to select at least three different tree leaves and, with the help of an adult or with their own knowledge, to identify the type of tree the leaf came from. Then ask them to bring the leaves to school and create a large collage on your bulletin board. Alongside the display, write the names of as many trees as possible. In addition, page 141 provides guidelines for identifying the living things that may be found on one tree.

- The book describes three basic types of trees: broadleaved, conifers, and palms. On separate paper, ask students to draw or find a picture in a magazine of each type of tree.

- Remind students that some trees look very different at different times of the year. Using a separate paper, each student selects a tree and describes how it looks in each of the four seasons. Ask them to write three sentences about their trees for each season.

- Trees come in all shapes and sizes. Some trees are very small while others have root systems that can take up an acre or more. Ask the children to use library books to identify some unusually-shaped trees. Page 142 asks students to identify the names of trees, the fruits or nuts that they produce, and then the products that can be made from those fruits or nuts.

- Ask students to select a tree either in their yard or one they pass by regularly. Ask them to keep a log on this tree for the entire school year, making at least one log entry each week. Use the cover provided on page 139. Tell students to consider the following points as they keep their logs:

    (A) How have the leaves changed?

    (B) How has the bark of the tree changed?

    (C) What kinds of animals or birds are in or near the tree?

    (D) How has the color changed?

    (E) How has the shape of the tree changed?

My Tree

_____
**Name**

**Name** _____**Date**_____

# Planting a Tree

**Directions:** Follow the steps outlined below to grow your own fruit tree. You will need a fruit seed, a coffee can, and some soil.

| | | |
|---|---|---|
| **Step 1:**<br><br>Remove the seed or seeds from the fruit. It is okay to have some fruit still attached to the seed, as this will nourish it.<br><br> | **Step 2:**<br><br>Place soil into your chosen container.<br><br> | **Step 3:**<br><br>Bury the seed about 4 to 6 inches below the top of the soil. Be sure it is completely covered.<br><br>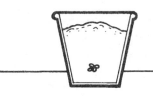 |
| **Step 4:**<br><br>Water the seed and put the container where it will get natural light. If it is summer, put the container outdoors.<br><br>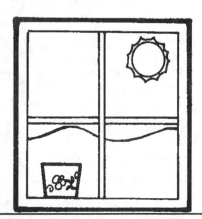 | **Step 5:**<br><br>Test the soil with your finger every few days for moisture. When the soil is dry, water it. Do not overwater.<br><br> | **Step 6:**<br><br>Watch your seedling grow. But don't be upset if the seed doesn't produce a tree. Each tree produces many, many seeds, and only a few turn into trees. Try again!<br><br> |

**Name** _____**Date**_____

# What's Alive?

**Directions:** Use the guidelines below to identify living things found on one tree. You will need a magnifying glass and a tape measure.

Identify a tree in your yard or neighborhood. Remember to focus on one tree only. Then, complete the following questions.

1. Watch your selected tree. How many animals do you see in the tree right now? List them.

   _____

   Continue to watch for several minutes. Now, how many animals have you seen? List them.

   _____

2. What are each of the animals doing in the tree?

   _____

3. What resources in the tree are they using?

   _____

4. How many birds have you counted? Name them.

   _____

5. Briefly describe the activities of the birds in the tree.

   _____

6. Now use your magnifying glass to look carefully at the trunk of the tree. Do you see any living things? What are they?

   _____

   Tell about your tree's dimensions:
   • Approximately how many feet high is it?

   _____

   • What is its circumference? (Use your measuring tape to measure around the tree.) _____

   • Approximately how many large branches does your tree have?

   _____

   • Can you guess the tree's age?

   _____

   On the back of this paper, draw a picture of your tree.

**Name** _____ **Date**_____

# Foods from Trees

**Directions:** In each column write the name of a tree, the fruit or nut it produces, and several food items that can be made from that fruit or nut. Some answers have already been provided as examples for you to complete.

| Tree Name | Fruit or Nut | Food Products |
|---|---|---|
| Acorn Tree | | |
| | Lemon | |
| | | Orange Juice |
| | Peach | |
| Palm Tree | | |
| | | Pecan Pie |
| Coconut Tree | | |
| | | Banana Split |
| | | Mango Shake |
| | | Apple Cider |
| Apricot Tree | | |

# Answer Key

**Page 9**

1. Sahara, Australian, Arabian, Namib, Gobi
2. Arabian, Gobi, Turkestan, Takla Makan
3. Sonora
4. Turkestan, Takla Makan, Sonoran, Kalahari
5. greater
6. Sahara, Kalahari, Namib; 10,750,000 Km²

**Page 17**

1. savannah
2. monsoon
3. predator
4. prairie
5. carnivores
6. herbivores
7. decomposers
8. arid region

**Page 21**

1. savanna
2. prairie
3. savanna
4. savanna
5. prairie
6. prairie
7. savanna

**Page 48**

A. 43%
B. 4%
C. 24%
D. 22%
E. 7%
1. 22%
2. 89%
3. Represents 7%; need to conserve

**Page 51**

1. 700,000
2. The oil disperses and spreads.
3. False
4. all living things, including birds, plants, urchins, and land animals who depend on the water for food

**Page 60**

1. sawgrass
2. preservation
3. poacher
4. hurricane
5. canal
6. Everglades or river of grass
7. ecology
8. homesteader
9. Marjory Stoneman Douglas
10. Answers will vary.

**Page 61**

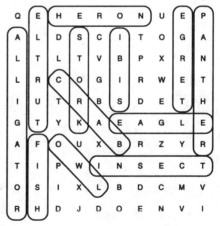

**Page 66**

A. 1
B. 6
C. 5
D. 2
E. 3
F. 4

# Answer Key *(cont.)*

## Page 67

## Page 86

1. blowhole
2. dorsal fin
3. flipper
4. fluke
5. herd
6. nostril
7. pod
8. sonar

## Page 89

1. below
2. 3.28
3. 13,612 feet
4. Pacific
5. Pacific
6. Arctic

## Page 100

1. Pacific, Atlantic, Indian, Southern, Arctic
2. Indian, Southern, Arctic
3. 120,857,000 and smaller
4. 13.56
5. 8,617,000 sq. mi.
6. 369,315,000

## Page 102

1. False
2. False
3. True
4. about 1/7
5. 924 gallons

## Page 106

## Page 119

1. I
2. F
3. B
4. G
5. D
6. E
7. H
8. C
9. A